THE CATHOLIC PRIEST
AS MORAL TEACHER AND GUIDE

THE CATHOLIC PRIEST
AS MORAL TEACHER AND GUIDE

Proceedings of a Symposium
Held at St. Charles Borromeo Seminary,
Overbrook, Pennsylvania

January 17–20, 1990

IGNATIUS PRESS   SAN FRANCISCO

#2295/936

Cover by Riz Boncan Marsella

With ecclesiastical approval
© 1990 Ignatius Press, San Francisco
ISBN 0-89870-312-3
Library of Congress catalogue number 90-82990
Printed in the United States of America

CONTENTS

FOREWORD

An important and instructive Symposium on Moral Theology and the Catholic Priesthood was held at St. Charles Seminary, Overbrook, Philadelphia, Pennsylvania on January 17–20, 1990.

The inaugural lecture, together with the concluding homily, was delivered by Joseph Cardinal Ratzinger outlining lucidly aspects of priestly formation—building a spiritual house, formed in God's family, learning and living a passion for truth and the Eucharist as the school of right living.

Both European and American scholars delivered substantive papers at this symposium: some scriptural roots of moral teaching (A. Vanhoye, S.J.) along with ministerial and ecclesiological aspects of that teaching (G. Chantraine, S.J.).

The need and importance of moral truths (W. E. May) and how correct moral teaching can help pastoral practice rather than injure it (G. Grisez) are clearly explained. The nature of priestly life is integrally linked with moral practice (J. Haas).

All these formal papers are accompanied by thoughtful and helpful responses. Any one of these contributions is worth reflective study, but all of them together provide a rich treasury of faithful and learned scholarship.

This symposium was held to inaugurate a new Chair in Moral Theology at the Philadelphia Seminary. The benefits of that Chair are already evident and real, and now fortunately available, in this publication—a rich benefit for any reader seriously interested in Catholic moral theology.

† John Cardinal O'Connor
Archbishop of New York

PREFACE

Shortly after his installation as Archbishop of Philadelphia on February 11, 1988, the Most Rev. Anthony Bevilacqua, J.C.D., J.D., decided to found a chair in moral theology at St. Charles Borromeo Seminary, Overbrook, in honor of his predecessor, John Cardinal Krol. Dr. John M. Haas was chosen to be the chair's first occupant, and Msgr. Daniel A. Murray, the rector, undertook the immense task of raising the funds necessary to endow the chair for perpetuity. Through the generosity of numerous contributors the chair has at last become a reality.

The idea of holding a symposium on the occasion of the chair's formal establishment seemed to all of us at St. Charles to be a fitting way both to honor Cardinal Krol and to mark the seminary's first endowed chair. The symposium was held January 17–20, 1990. We express our gratitude to each of the speakers and especially to Joseph Cardinal Ratzinger, Prefect of the Congregation for the Doctrine of the Faith, who gave the keynote address and participated in all of the symposium sessions. Cardinal Ratzinger also preached a homily at St. Charles Borromeo Seminary on the day following the symposium. We have included this homily in the present volume.

Monsignor Thomas Herron
St. Charles Borromeo Seminary

ix

CONTRIBUTORS

Dr. J. Brian Benestad, Professor of Political Theory and Social Ethics in the Department of Theology and Religious Studies, University of Scranton.

Fr. Georges Chantraine, S.J., Professor of Dogmatic Theology at the University of Namur and Peritus at the 1987 Synod of Bishops in Rome on the role of the laity.

Dr. Germain Grisez, Flynn Professor of Christian Ethics, Mount St. Mary's College, Emmitsburg, Maryland.

Dr. John M. Haas, John Cardinal Krol Professor of Moral Theology, St. Charles Borromeo Seminary, Overbrook.

Rev. Msgr. Thomas J. Herron, S.T.D., S.S.L., Professor of Dogmatic Theology and Sacred Scripture, St. Charles Borromeo Seminary, Overbrook, Pennsylvania.

Rev. Msgr. Richard K. Malone, S.T.D., J.C.L., Co-director, Cambridge Center for the Study of Faith and Culture, Cambridge, Massachusetts.

Dr. William E. May, Professor of Moral Theology, Catholic University of America, Washington, D.C., and member of the International Theological Commission.

Rev. Kevin T. McMahon, S.T.D., Professor of Moral Theology, St. Charles Borromeo Seminary, Overbrook.

Rev. Msgr. James J. Mulligan, S.T.D., Pastor and former Professor of Moral Theology, Mount St. Mary's Seminary, Emmitsburg, Maryland.

Joseph Cardinal Ratzinger, Prefect of the Congregation for the Doctrine of the Faith, former Archbishop of Munich, Professor of Dogmatic Theology in numerous state universities of Germany, and Peritus at Vatican II.

FR. ALBERT VANHOYE, S.J., Professor and Rector of the Pontifical Biblical Institute, Rome, and member of the Pontifical Biblical Commission.

INTRODUCTION

For reasons best known to himself, two years ago the Lord decided that Father Hans Urs von Balthasar did not need to be made a cardinal, and so he called the father to himself. Perhaps the College needed no more distinguished members. Perhaps Father von Balthasar needed no other honors on earth.

Whatever the case, Father von Balthasar wrote this shortly before he died:

> The only question that the Church should ask herself is the following: How should I look so that humanity can see the true Christ through me? . . . Nobody will ever convert to Christ because of a Magisterium, sacraments, a clergy, canon law, apostolic nunciatures or a gigantic ecclesiastical machinery. Conversion will occur when a person encounters a Catholic who communicates the Christian message with his life and thus testifies that there exists not *a* but *the* believable imitation of Christ within the Catholic sphere. The Council expressed this lucidly in *Dei Verbum,* no. 10, by referring to the indivisibility of the three elements: Sacred Scripture, Tradition and the Church's Magisterium. These are the conditions under which the entire people of God can attain holiness and thus become a believable witness to Jesus Christ.[1]

For the Catholic theologian, the Second Vatican Council has thus concisely explained the inner logic of Catholic theology's method. If it is unthinkable for the physicist to do his work without using the findings of the great heroes of his science who went before him, so must theologians locate themselves and their work within the great heritage of the community of faith, expressed best in Sacred Scripture, the Word of the Lord, the living God.

[1] Hans Urs von Balthasar, *Test Everything: Hold Fast to What Is Good* (San Francisco: Ignatius Press, 1989), 17–18.

But it is naïve to think that the Scripture is ever understood without being interpreted. And ultimately it is meaningless to claim that the Church enjoys the guidance of an indwelling Holy Spirit if there are no sensible results of such guidance. In other words, if there is no Spirit-led Magisterium, perhaps it is untrue after all that the Spirit has been given to those who have encountered the Risen Lord. If, on the other hand, a holy spirit of truth *has* been given to us who believe, it is not odd that a Magisterium should be generated within our community. We have had teachers to help us learn. Some think that very strange. I would say the opposite: it would be strange if we claimed to have learned something and could not identify who our teachers were.

To discuss the Scripture in light of the Tradition and the Magisterium, then, is not to distort the written Word of the Lord; rather, it is to attend clearly to the method that one's interpretation employs. It is only when that method is openly admitted that it can be honestly examined.

The symposium was entitled "The Catholic Priest as Moral Teacher and Guide". This was done deliberately, not only to provide a forum in which this important theme would be discussed, but also to provide an instance, an experiment if you will, in which the three fundamental elements of Catholic theology, as outlined by *Dei Verbum,* no. 10, could clearly be seen at work. Although we are here printing the major addresses of the symposium, considerable emphasis was given to a discussion of the theme's many aspects. Naturally, these "Proceedings" could include only the principal contributions.

It is to be noted that the "priest" is the *Catholic* priest. At least in part it seems that the continuing drift in understanding the identity of the priest is due to a certain reluctance to say we are speaking of the Catholic priest, in a real, historical, organically continuous community of faith, which Saint Paul would repeatedly describe as nothing other than the Body of Christ. This does not deny or suppress an ecumenical dimension: it makes effective ecumenical dialogue possible because it is more honest and more real.

The theme is further specified by emphasizing the dimension of morality. This was done, not simply because the symposium marked the formal foundation of a chair in moral theology, but also because it was thought that the present crisis in moral theology warranted just such special attention. The crisis, it ought to be said at last, is unprecedented in the degree to which the moral doctrine of the Catholic Church is actively opposed and denied *by Catholics.* The Reformation thought the Roman Church *lax.* If she is vilified today for being rigorous, the least that can be said is that something has changed and changed dramatically.

At the point we are at today, many theologians deny that the Church even *has* a coherent moral doctrine that she can legitimately teach and preach. This is because many who dissent from the moral teaching of the Church defend themselves by saying that they have not, in so doing, touched anything belonging to the core of the Faith. But surely Christianity from the beginning has meant adopting a certain set of distinctive mores. The first expression of the Gospel in Mark is in the word *metanoiete,* "be converted". But be converted from what, to what?

Others, with an incoherence one suspects is not entirely recognized, complain that the Church's moral doctrine—for example, on social justice questions—is not being accorded the reception it deserves among Catholics. But if the Church is unreliable in one area of moral doctrine, how trustworthy is she likely to be in others?

The theme singles out two aspects, teacher and guide, for particular study. They are meant to suggest a profound complementarity between what is taught theoretically, so to speak, and how this is lived out on a more practical level, the level of pastoral care. It echoes the coupling between *de fide* and *de moribus* in the classical expression of the content of the Church's teaching.

In planning the program, then, we tried to take seriously the advice that Father von Balthasar offered. The speakers included authorities on Scripture, dogmatic theology and moral theology. They combined insights drawn from the biblical literature, from the Church's Tradition and from the pronouncements of the

Magisterium. In bringing these Proceedings to the public, we can only hope they will be of help to all in the Church who believe that not just *a* but *the* imitation of Christ can be lived in her.

Rev. Msgr. Thomas J. Herron, S.T.D., S.S.L.
Professor of Sacred Scripture and
  Dogmatic Theology
St. Charles Borromeo Seminary, Overbrook

JOSEPH CARDINAL RATZINGER

Keynote Address

SOME PERSPECTIVES ON PRIESTLY FORMATION TODAY

In his first Holy Thursday letter to the bishops of the Church, our present Holy Father wrote: "The full reconstitution of the life of the seminaries throughout the Church will be the best proof of the achievement of the renewal to which the Council directed the Church." I was happy to learn that on October 3, 1979, His Holiness repeated those same words in this very chapel of St. Charles Seminary, on the occasion of his first pastoral visit to the United States. I feel confident, then, that my theme, "Some Perspectives on Priestly Formation Today", is an appropriate subject to discuss. You know that it is the theme of the next synod of bishops.

When Archbishop Bevilacqua invited me to come to Philadelphia and to speak at the opening of this symposium, "The Catholic Priest as Moral Teacher and Guide", I could think of no better beginning for such a meeting than to discuss priestly formation. Likewise I was sure that it was a fitting topic because I know of Cardinal Krol's own great interest in the seminary and in the education of his priests. May I also offer him my best wishes as the new chair in moral theology is founded in his honor.

I

TO BE BUILT UP INTO A SPIRITUAL HOUSE:
BEING FORMED INTO GOD'S FAMILY

When I was appointed archbishop of Munich and Freising in 1977, I saw that I had been placed in a situation of crisis and ferment. Those preparing for the priesthood in the archdiocese had become few; they were housed in the seminary of the Georgianum that Duke George, called the "Rich", had founded in 1494 to be the Bavarian regional seminary at the University of Ingolstadt, later moved to Munich. It was clear to me from the start that it was my pressing duty to give the diocese its own seminary for the training of priests again, even if many were doubtful whether such a project would still be meaningful given the changes in the Church. Shortly before I was called upon to leave my home diocese once again to take up my present responsibilities, on November 20, 1981, the feast of Saint Korbinian, the diocesan Patron, a day threatening with rain, it was my joy to lay the cornerstone for a seminary building that, with its lines reaching upward, was already impressive. Thus, a beginning at least had been made from which there was no turning back; it had to go forward. When I thought about what words should be inscribed on the cornerstone, I was struck by the wonderful verse from the first letter of Peter wherein Israel's titles of honor were applied to those made a people by baptism: "As living stones, let yourselves be built into a spiritual house, a holy priesthood to offer spiritual sacrifices pleasing to God through Jesus Christ" (1 P 2:5). These words probably formed part of a New Testament catechetical instruction on baptism. They apply to the new community of Jesus Christ, the theology of the Covenant and of the Election, with which the Sinai event in the Old Testament was interpreted. Thus we have a simple description of what it means to be one of the baptized and how the Church, God's living house, grows in the world. But what could really take place in a seminary that would be nobler or better than that young men in the power of their baptism grow in discipleship, than that they indeed become parts of the living Church? It seemed to me, then, that the words of Saint Peter to the baptized said all that was necessary as far as a seminary was concerned, that they could rightly be looked upon as a mission statement, as the cornerstone for such a house.

Why should we have a seminary? How should the formation of priests proceed today? In our Scripture text, we find first of all a reference to the building of a spiritual house out of living stones. *House* in the biblical sense of the term denotes not so much a building of stones but kith and kin, the family. This usage continues among us even today when we speak about a noble house—the house of Wittelsbach or Habsburg, et cetera.[1] The baptized who are originally strangers to one another are to become one family, God's family. This is a process that ought to find concrete application in the seminary so that the future priest develops the ability in his parish, or wherever he may be, to bring people together into the family, into the community of God's house. To be sure, there is still the qualification—a *spiritual* house. This does not mean, as our feeling for language might suggest, a house in a merely figurative and thus unreal and imaginary sense. Here the word *spiritual* is derived from the Holy Spirit and from his creative power, without which nothing is real at all. A spiritual house built by the Holy Spirit is first and foremost the truly real house. The belonging to one another that stems from the Holy Spirit reaches deeper and is stronger and more lively than the simple kinship of blood. All those who have been touched by the Holy Spirit are brought together, stand in closer solidarity than any other kind of relationship could establish. John's Gospel speaks in this context about those who believe in the name of the Logos and who thus receive a new origin: "born not by blood, nor by the will of the flesh, nor by the will of man but from God" (Jn 1:13). Here the connection is made with the very One who was conceived, not by the will of the flesh, but by the power of

---

[1] Cf. O. Michel, *OEKOS KTd,* ThWNT, V, 122–61, esp. 113f.; H. A. Hoffner, "hajit" in *Theol. Worterbuch zum AT,* I, 629–38; M. Wodke, "Oikos in der Septuaginta. Erste Grundlagen", in *Hebraica,* ed. O. Rossler (Berlin, 1977), 59–140, esp. 60ff.

the Holy Spirit, Jesus Christ. We are the "spiritual house" if we are the house and the members of the family of Jesus Christ. This brings an inner harmony, a new seal and a new foundation for life that is stronger than all differences and permits new, interior kinship to mature. The seminary, like the Church and like every family, is in continual development. This is the only way in which it fully comes about, namely, that men allow themselves to be built up into a living house by Jesus Christ.

And so we might now say quite simply that the essential task of the seminary is to offer a space wherein this spiritual building-up can take place over and over again. Its task is to be a place for meeting Jesus Christ, an encounter that so unites men with him that they can become his voice in the present for others and for the world of today. This basic statement becomes more concrete if we return once again to our text. The end is the house; what goes before it are the stones—living stones that go into a living house. Now it should be noted that the reference to building in our passage appears in the passive: as living stones, let yourselves be built into a spiritual house. In accordance with our urge to be doing something, we completely transpose these words into the active: to build the kingdom of God, to build the Church, to build a new society, et cetera. The New Testament views our role in another way. The builder is God himself or the Holy Spirit. We are the stones; the building, as far as we are concerned, is a "being built". The traditional hymn for the liturgy of the consecration of a church describes this in a forceful way when it speaks of the healing marks of the chisel, the manifold works wrought by the Master's hammer and the decorous assembly, by which the blocks of stone are finally brought together to grow into the great building of the new Jerusalem. Something quite important is touched on here: *building* means "being built". If we want to be the house, each one of us has to take upon himself the destiny of being well prepared. In order to be of use for the house, we have to let ourselves be properly formed for the place where we are needed. The one who wishes to be part of the whole vast array and become a stone set in it has to allow himself to be united to the whole. He can no longer simply do or act as the thought occurs to him and it seems the thing to do. He can no longer simply go where he wants. He has to accept the fact that it is another who girds him and leads him where he would not go (cf. Jn 21:18). In John's Gospel, we find still another figure: the vine that has to produce fruit must be pruned; it has to allow itself to be clipped. The process of bearing greater fruit is experienced only by accepting the pain of being pruned, purified (Jn 15:2).

In consequence, we can be sure that the formation of priests has to offer more than a professional training: an education in proper living as a human being. Furthermore, it has first and foremost to provide for the acquiring of those fundamental virtues without which no family can long remain united. This is so important for the priest because not only must he be ready to live together with the family of his presbyterate, his local Church and the Church universal, but his task, over and above this, is to bring and hold together in the community of faith those who are strangers to one another by reason of origin, education, temperament and the circumstances of life. He has to lead people to reconciliation, to be able to forgive and to forget, to forbearance and magnanimity. He has to help each bear with the other in his otherness, to have patience with the other and to exhibit in proper balance trust and prudence, discretion and openness, and much more besides. He must be ready before all else to stand by people in their tribulations—both in physical sufferings and in the disappointments, adversities and worries of which no one is spared. How should he do all this if he himself has not learned it first of all? To be able to accept and endure suffering is one of the basic requirements for human happiness; when this is not learned, life is bound to fail. Being provoked with everyone and everything dries up the soil of the soul, so to speak, and makes it a wasteland. Formerly we used to speak of the mastery of pain in connection with asceticism. This word is no longer used today; we come nearer to its meaning when we translate it from the Greek into English: "training". Everyone knows that there can be no success without training and its corresponding mastery of the self. For every possible art today people train themselves with zeal and concentration, and thus peaks of achievement are attainable in many areas that in former times would have been unthinkable. But why does it seem so farfetched to be in training for real, genuine living? To practice the art of renunciation, of self mastery, of inner freedom from our addictions?

THE PASSION FOR TRUTH

Among the many things that might be said here, I would like to raise one point in particular: to educate in the truth. The truth often makes people uncomfortable; it is probably the strictest of teachers in the process of learning unselfishness and real freedom. Let us take the example of Pilate. He knows for a fact that the accused Jesus is innocent and that, according to justice, he should acquit him. He even wants to do so. But then this truth begins to conflict with his position; it threatens him with inconvenience, even with the loss of his post. Public disturbances could arise; he may be made to appear in an unfavorable light with Caesar. These and similar fears arise. And so he prefers to sacrifice the truth, which neither cries out nor defends itself, even if its betrayal leaves behind in his soul the dull ache of failure. This situation constantly recurs in history: we need only call to mind a further example that is the reverse of the preceding one—Thomas More. How natural it seemed that the king should be accorded supremacy over the Church. There was no formulation of dogma that clearly excluded it. All the bishops had accepted it; why should he, a layman, put his life at risk and plunge his family into ruin? If he would no longer think of himself, in weighing the values ought he not at least give priority to his dear ones over this obstinate insistence upon following his conscience? Cases like these portray in large dimensions, if you will, only what our own lives witness again and again in smaller ways. I can extract myself from some difficulty if I make a small concession to dishonesty. Or to put it the other way: accepting the consequences of the truth will not necessarily lessen the difficulties in which I find myself. How often does this happen? And how often do we fail! The situation in which Thomas More found himself when it is translated into daily experience goes like this: lots of people say this is all right; why not me too? Why should I upset the harmony of the group? Why make myself the object of ridicule? Does not society's peace take precedence over my own rights? In this way, group conformity leads to tyranny over the truth. Georges Bernanos, whose life was not spared the mystery of the priestly vocation and the tragedy of its failure, dramatically portrayed the perils involved in the figure of Bishop Espelette. This well-liked bishop had been a professor; he is knowledgeable and amiable; he always knows what to say, just what the situation calls for and what the educated world expects from a bishop in his position.

> The courage of this clever priest, however, deceives no one but himself. His intellectual cowardice is huge. . . . No one is less worthy of love than one who lives only for the sake of being loved. Souls of this kind, so deft that they change themselves according to each man's taste, are only mirrors.

Bernanos pursues his analysis of this failure all the way to its core:

> "I am a man of my time", he keeps repeating with the look of a man who doesn't toot his own horn. . . . But he never paid any attention to the fact that each time he would say this he was disowning the eternal character with which he had been sealed.[2]

I am not standing up to be counted among those who decry the great sickness of our time as the scarcity of truth. In effect, events have gone beyond this everywhere. What remains evident is the disavowal of the truth and the flight into group conformity as the way to peace. A community like this is built on sand. The pain associated with the truth is a prerequisite for real community. It has to be accepted day after day. It is only with truth's little acts

[2] Georges Bernanos, *L'imposture* (Bibliotheque de la Pleiade, 1961), 387–88.

of patience that we ripen from within and become free from ourselves, free for God.

Here is the place where our image of the living stones emerges once again. Peter illustrates the interior call that this image raises with a passage from Psalms 118:22, which has long since been understood as one of the basic christological texts: "The stone rejected by the builders has become the cornerstone." We are not interested here in following in detail the theology of death and Resurrection that lies hidden in this verse. But its association with the idea of the living stone has already brought us to recognize that building involves a being built, that without this passive attitude the passion of purification cannot take place. Bernanos regarded pain as of the essence of the Divine Heart, and thus he considered most precious all the bodily and spiritual sufferings that the Lord sends us.[3] The rejected stone is a figure for him who took upon himself the mortal pain of radical love and thus opened up a place for all of us, becoming the cornerstone that founds a living house, a new family out of fractured humanity. In the seminary, when it comes to the training of priests, we do not form just *any* kind of group. If we did, there would be the danger that the pain of becoming a part of it would go only to the point of conformity whereby we sacrifice the truth. We do not build according to a self-set standard. We allow ourselves to be made a part of the building by him who is our model and ideal, by the second Adam whom Paul calls a life-giving Spirit (1 Co 15:45). This building plan justifies the hardships of purification and gives us a guarantee that it *is* purification and not destruction. A person grows into this building when he seeks to acquire "everything that is true, noble, good, pure, worthy of love and honorable, everything virtuous and worthy of praise" (Ph 4:8). A person becomes right for the building when he becomes true.

When this goal is achieved, the seminary becomes a home. Without this common path it would be no more than a collection of student rooms whose occupants ultimately remain each on his

[3] Ibid., 352.

own. Being prepared to be purified even guarantees that such a house will have its share of humor and cheerfulness. Without it the atmosphere becomes chiefly one of griping and complaints against everyone, including oneself. In such an atmosphere, the days are gray and joy cannot grow because it does not have the sunshine it needs to ripen.

HOUSE AND TEMPLE:
SERVING THE INCARNATE WORD

These considerations open our way to a second reflection, in which we can now speak about training for the priestly vocation beyond the essential formation of the human being and the Christian. Our passage on the spiritual house built of living stones once again provides us with a starting point. This is the house that God builds for himself in the world and that we at the same time build for him—"God's house". The whole theology of the Temple is taken up in this term. The Temple is first of all the place of God's dwelling, the space of his presence in the world. It is therefore the place of the assembly within which the Covenant is renewed over and over again. It is the place where God meets his people and where they also find themselves. It is the place from which God's Word proceeds, the spot where the standard of his wisdom is raised and from which it becomes visible. It is ultimately, then, the place of God's glory. It shines forth in the inviolable purity of his Word. It shines forth, too, in the festive beauty of the liturgical act. Glory manifests itself in the act of glorifying, which is the response to the call of his Word—a response that concentrates and anticipates, which then has to be continued in the active language of all of one's life, which should be the reflection of his glory. The rending of the curtain of the Temple at the moment of Jesus' death on the Cross signified that this building had ceased to be the place where God and man meet in this world. From the moment of Jesus' death, his body given for us is the new and true

Temple; the subsequent destruction of the temple of stone in the year 70 only makes visible to the eyes of all history what had already occurred in the death of Jesus.[4] Now is the verse of the psalm completely fulfilled: "Sacrifice and oblations you wished not, but a body you have prepared for me" (Ps 40:6; Heb 10:5). Worship has now acquired a new and definitive meaning: we glorify God when we become one body with Christ; that means a new, spiritual existence in which he embraces us totally, body and life (cf. 1 Co 6:17). We glorify God when we allow ourselves to be drawn into that act of love that he accomplished on the Cross. Glorification and Covenant, worship and life become inseparably one. The hour of Jesus, which lasts now until the end of days, consists in this: that from the Cross he draws us to himself (Jn 12:32) so that we can become "one" with him (Ga 3:28).

In this new worship, which occurs in the Easter Passover from ourselves to the place of Christ's body, the essential elements that determined the cult of the Old Testament continue to hold good; only now, for the first time, do they attain their full meaning. *Temple,* as we said, is first of all the place of God's Word. Thus, the priesthood that stands at the service of the Incarnate Word has to make God's Word present in its unadulterated purity and its everlasting reality. It is essential that the priest of the New Covenant not present just any personal philosophy of life that he thinks good or has read about, but the Word that has been entrusted to our faithful hands and that we may not tamper with, as Paul states forcefully and clearly in the second letter to the Corinthians (2:17). Here we find ourselves before the challenging responsibility to which the priest must set himself; behind it the breadth and depth of what priestly formation and training mean become clear. As a priest, I may not present my personal ideas for I am sent by Another, and that alone gives importance to my message. "We are ambassadors for Christ, and God it is who is appealing through us. We beg you in Christ's name: be reconciled with God!" (2 Co

---

[4] Cf. W. Trilling, *Christusverkundigung in den synoptischen Evangelien* (Munich, 1968), 201; J. Gnilka, *Das Matthausevangelium,* pt. II (Freiburg, 1988), 476.

5:20). It is this statement of Paul that remains the true definition of what is the fundamental form and mission of priestly existence in the Church of the New Covenant. I have to deliver the Word of Another and that means first of all: I have to come to know it; I have to have understood it; it must become my own.

This proclamation, however, requires much more than the attitude of a messenger with a telegram who faithfully delivers strange words that mean nothing to him. I have to hand on the Word of Another in the first person, in a quite personal way and so appropriate it to myself that it becomes my own word. For this message does not require a telegrapher but a witness. While a person usually forms his thought and then looks for the right word, the reverse is true here: the Word goes before him. He puts himself at its disposal and gives himself to the Word. In this process of coming to know, to understand, to enter into and to become familiar with the Word, we find the essence of all training for the priesthood. In his book of exercises, Father Kolvenbach calls this subordination of one's learning to the teaching of the Church a *sacrificium intellectus* and then goes on to say:

> This sacrifice stamps upon one's spiritual effort . . . the mark of an offering in the true sense of the word and thus of a priestly seal upon . . . the ability . . . to preach; it does not depend . . . primarily upon knowledge but upon the immersion of his understanding in the vaster wisdom of God's Word. Just as for the Levites, the prophets, and the apostles, there is for the preachers of God's Word a process of learning—one which never ends. In it one gives first place to the honor of God. . . . A priest has to dedicate himself unreservedly to the Word of God.[5]

Father Kolvenbach here explains the mysterious phrase of Saint Paul, that we have to "put on Christ": the putting on of Christ consists in the process of our identification with the Word of faith, having an interior familiarity with this Word, in order that it becomes our very own because we have become its own.

[5] Hans Kolvenbach, *Der osterliche Weg: Exerzitien zur Lebenserneuerung* (Freiburg, 1989), 24.

Practically speaking, this means that in the study of theology the intellectual and the spiritual dimensions are inseparable from each other. That God's Word might be accessible to us in this world, that God has said something to us and is speaking still, is truly the most exciting news I can think of; but by habit we are so blasé that we advert only to the extraordinary in such revelation. Recently, I became acquainted with a little story that Helmut Thielicke relates in his memoirs. Two philology students, who had never had any kind of religious instruction, attended a sermon he preached in Hamburg's Church of St. Michael. What impressed them most of all was the common recitation at the end of the Our Father, whose words they had never learned. Because everyone seemed to know it, they didn't venture to ask about it but set themselves to researching the matter. Their effort to find it in the public library failed. Even in the library of the theology faculty they couldn't locate the text. The matter became ever more perplexing for them until finally, during a Sunday broadcast of a morning religious service, they were able to write down the Our Father as it was prayed in common over the air. "So at last we had the Our Father in hand", they both concluded in relating to Thielicke their long and arduous search to find the Lord's Prayer, which ultimately ended in their conversion to the Catholic Church.[6] Right in our present time we have a repetition of what the Lord had to observe in the gentiles' coming to faith: "I have not found such faith in Israel" (Mt 8:10). The adventure of coming to recognize the closeness of God's word in all its exciting beauty and of entering into it with all one's powers belongs to the essence of the priestly vocation. For this reason, no effort to come to know God's word can be too much. If it is worth the trouble to learn Italian in order to appreciate Dante in the original, how much more obvious it should be for us to learn to read the Scriptures in their original languages. Every care for historical study obviously accompanies our expedition into God's Word. A

---

[6] Helmut Thielicke, *Zu Gast auf einem schonen Stern. Erinnerungen* (Hamburg, 1984), 307ff.

rational education, training in methodical work, is an indispensable element on the path to the priesthood. One who loves wants to learn. He can never know enough about the one he loves. Concern for learning is thus an inner demand of love. A methodical education, by the way, one that constantly affords a person the chance to discard his pet theories for the sake of obedience, is an indispensable means of training in the truth and in truthfulness, an essential ingredient for the objectivity of any witness who does not proclaim himself but places himself wholly at the service of One who is greater. A piety that tries to evade this ends up with just feeling. Building without the truth is a kind of spiritual self-abuse to which we may not succumb.

A careful and educated effort to understand Holy Scripture is the foundation for training in the priesthood. But it should be obvious that a merely historical reading of Scripture is not enough. We do not read it as a word of men from the past; we read it as God's Word, which he, through the men of a bygone age, permits to be addressed to all ages as his ever new and present Word. To let the Word dwell merely in the past is to deny that the Bible is the Bible. The kind of historical interpretation that merely dwells on what was brings in its consequence the denial of the canon and, to that extent, a refusal to accept the Bible as the Bible. To accept the canon of Scripture already means in itself to take the Word beyond its simple historical moment; it means the recognition of God's people as the continual bearer of the Word and the Author among the authors. Since, however, no people is God's people on its own, the acceptance of this Agent means at the same time a recognition that it is God who is at work in and through them as the genuine inspirator of their ways and of their memory set to writing. Exegesis becomes biblical exegesis and theology when it operates from this perspective; theology arises from the fact that there is this common Agent, the Church; without this Agent there is no theology.[7] When the Church is left out, theology

---

[7] See Joseph Ratzinger, *Schriftauslegung im Widerstreit* (Freiburg, 1989), esp. 7–44; on the question of the Church as "subject" of theology I would make reference to my essay, "Theology and Church" in *Internat. Kath. Zeitschr.* 15 (1986), 515–33.

becomes the philosophy of religion: the scientific pursuit of theology disintegrates into a variety of concurrent disciplines—historical, philosophical and practical—in the same way that the canon disintegrates when there is no continual Agent who alone can justify it as the canon. When the interior presence of this Church-Agent weakens in souls, the process of disintegration is at work: the dissolution of the canon and theology as theology are ineluctably part of a series of disciplines barely connected to one another. This is the great temptation of our day when the understanding of the Church-Mystery is almost completely extinguished and the universal Church is regarded generally as just an organizational carrier that can coordinate things of religious importance but that does not enter into religion itself. Religion takes place only in the midst of community. For this reason, the experience of and the acceptance of the Church are an essential component of priestly formation. If the Church does not "awaken in souls" at this time, then everything remains subjective. Faith becomes a personal choice regarding what seems possible for me; the process of self-renunciation and absorption in the Word of Another does not occur. The Word ultimately remains my word. I do not yield myself to the Body of Christ but stay all to myself.

This means that an obvious necessity for the priesthood is an academic formation that is both comprehensive and versatile. The religion of the Logos is by its nature a rational religion. It likewise has its philosophical and historical dimensions for it is immersed in the concrete; all this, however, can come together only if there is a truly theological center that cannot exist without the reality of the Church. Today, in this age of growing specialization, the search for the interior unity of theology and concentration upon its center seem to me to have become an urgent priority. A theologian certainly must develop versatility, but theology itself must be ever capable of shifting ballast and directing its concentration upon the essential. Theology needs to be able to differentiate between specialized knowledge and the fundamentals; above all else it has to mediate an organic vision of the whole in which the essential is integrated. If so-called specialization goes so far that in the end there is an assortment of unconnected specialized fields, it has missed the mark. Only with a vision of the whole can we recognize those indispensable criteria for the discernment that is so necessary for the spiritual leader and for the preacher's spiritual independence. If he does not learn to judge with a view to the whole, then he is ever consigned as a prey to changing fashions.

I come now to another aspect. It has always given me pause for reflection that in the Roman canon of the Mass when priests pray for themselves, we find they are called by the name "sinners": *nobis quoque peccatoribus.* This official self-designation on the part of the clergy in the sight of God has nothing to do with worthiness; it goes right to the heart: we are "sinful servants".[8] I don't believe that we can attribute this simply to some empty show of humility. Here is expressed the selfsame consciousness that Isaiah exclaimed in the presence of God's vision: "Woe is me; I am lost. For I am a man of unclean lips . . . and my eyes have seen the King, the Lord of hosts" (6:5); the selfsame consciousness that made Peter fall to his knees when he saw the miraculous catch of fish and say, "Depart from me, Lord, for I am a sinful man" (Lk 5:8); the selfsame consciousness that found expression in the old ordination liturgy when the bishop instructed the candidates: "With great fear should one ascend to such a grade". It is danger-ous to bring oneself close to the everlasting presence of the Holy, which can easily become routine for me and ordinary and then burdensome. The hard words of Jesus to the pharisees and the priests touch upon a basic psychological and sociological phe-nomenon that constantly occurs: routine makes dull. We may think again, for example, of our two students on their search for the Our Father, in which we saw the desire of the gentiles and our own blindness. Because of this, the Church in the past constantly emphasized that you cannot study theology simply as a profession like any other, for then we would be dealing with God's Word as though it were a thing that belongs to us. But that is not the case.

[8] Cf. J. A. Jungmann, *Missarum sollemnia,* II (Freiburg, 1952), 311; T. Schnitzler, *Die Messe in der Betrachtung,* I (Freiburg, 1955), 104f.

Moses had to take off his shoes before the burning bush. We also might say: whoever exposes himself to the radioactive ray of God's Word—indeed, whoever handles it as his vocation—must be prepared to live close to such a presence else he will be burned. One can see how real this danger is, for it is probable that all the great crises in the Church were essentially connected to a decline in the clergy, for whom intercourse with the Holy had ceased to be the fascinating and perilous mystery it is, of coming close to the burning presence of the All-Holy One, and had become instead a comfortable craft by which to secure one's daily needs. The venture of being called close to the mystery of God requires a preparation like that of Moses, who heard words that still hold true: one must take off one's shoes. Shoes made of leather, from the skins of dead animals, were a symbol of the dead, of that from which we must free ourselves in order to be able to live in the presence of the One who is life. The dead—this is first of all the excess of dead things, possessions, with which a man surrounds himself. The dead also refers to those behaviors that oppose the paschal way of life: only the one who loses himself finds himself. The priesthood demands a departure from bourgeois existence; it has to incorporate within itself in a methodical way this losing of one's self. The Church's joining of celibacy and the priesthood brings out these considerations: celibacy stands in starkest contradiction to the normal fulfillment of life. When a man accepts it interiorly, he cannot look upon the priesthood as one professional attainment among others. Instead he must somehow assent to the renunciation of his own life's aspirations and allow himself to be girded and led where he really would rather not go. Before entering into such a decision, the Word of the Lord has to be heard and reflected upon: "If one of you intends to build a tower, would he not first sit down and reckon the cost to see if he had means enough to complete it?" (Lk 14:28). No one can choose the priesthood for himself to fulfill his own life. A basic requirement for the priesthood is a careful discernment of whether I am responding to the Lord's call or am only looking for self-fulfillment. The requirement to keep in vital contact with him remains constant all along the path. For if we turn our glance from him, what happened to Peter when he met Jesus walking on the water will surely happen to us. Only the look of the Lord can overpower gravity, but he really can do it. We ever remain sinners. But when he takes hold of us, the waters of the deep lose their power.

In this context, I would like once again to return to the *nobis quoque,* the prayer of the priest in the Roman canon. In behalf of the priest, it calls upon those who have gone before him on the way, the intercessors; at their head is John the Baptist, and following upon him are two groups of seven saints: seven men, all martyrs, and seven holy women and virgins. They cover the diverse geographical areas of the Church, and they embody the various vocations in the Church, all of God's holy people.[9] The priest is directed toward the support given by the saints and the whole living community of the faithful. It strikes me as especially significant that the Roman canon calls upon the names of holy women precisely in its prayer for priests. Priestly celibacy has nothing to do with misogyny. Nor does it mean having no association with women. The process of a priest's interior growth depends quite essentially upon his finding a proper relationship with women; he needs the support given by mothers, virgins, career women, widows, who accept his special calling and accompany him in it with a selfless, pure feminine goodness and concern.

WORD AND SACRAMENT—THE PLACE OF WORSHIP

Our considerations bring us back once again to the thought that we should be built into the living temple. To the temple belong liturgy and sacrifice—this is what the first letter of Peter tells us. As Christians, we believe in the Word who became man. For this reason priestly service must reach beyond mere sermons, beyond the simple interpretation of the Scripture: what has become mani-

[9] See Schnitzler, *Die Messe in der Betrachtung,* 105.

fest with the Word has passed over into the sacraments, Saint Leo the Great once observed.[10] The word of faith is essentially a sacramental Word. By its nature, training for the priesthood must be a preparation for the service of the sacraments, the Church's sacramental liturgy. I do not intend now to describe at length what this means because all that has been said up to this point has been a quiet reflection of the sacramental perspective. One thing is clear: the daily Eucharist has to be the heart of any formation for the priesthood. The chapel must constitute the center of the seminary, and staying close to the Eucharist has to be continued and deepened by personal prayer in the presence of the Lord. The sacrament of penance must be, so to speak, the burning coal of purification of which the Prophet Isaiah speaks in relating the vision in which he received his vocation (6:6); it has to be this power of reconciliation by which the Lord leads us, over and over again, from all manner of division into unity.

Silence belongs to the liturgy just as much as festivity. When I think back to my own years in the seminary, the moments of morning Mass with their inexhaustible freshness and purity, along with the grand liturgies celebrated with full festive splendor, remain my loveliest memories. The liturgy just by itself is beautiful; we ourselves are not the actors in it. Rather, we enter into that which is greater, that which embraces us and takes us for its own. Still once more I would like to go back to the Roman canon of the Mass: in the *communicantes,* the eucharistic prayer calls upon the names of twenty-four saints, a quiet reflection of the twenty-four elders who in the vision of the Apocalypse surround God's throne in the heavenly liturgy.[11] Every liturgy is cosmic in its dimensions, a stepping out from our poor little groupings into the great community that spans earth and heaven. This is what gives it its breadth, its great vitality. This is what makes every liturgy a feast. It is this that renders our silence precious and, at the same time,

---

[10] *Sermo. 2,* "De Ascensione", 2 PL 54, 398.

[11] Schnitzler, *Die Messe in der Betrachtung,* 76; on the nature of the liturgy see J. Corbon, *Liturgie aus dem Urquell* (Einsiedeln, 1981).

challenges us to enlist the service of every created thing that may aid our joining in the song of the eternal choir.

Cult has to do with culture—the connection here is obvious. Culture loses its soul without cult; cult without culture mistakes its true worth. If preparation for the priesthood is essentially at its heart a liturgical training, then a seminary needs to be a house wherein a wide-ranging cultural formation is provided. Music, literature, the arts delight in nature—all these have a place here. There are various gifts, and the nice thing about it is that in the seminary many and diverse gifts can be brought together in one. No one can do everything, but no one should resign himself to being uncultured. In the liturgy, we touch the Beautiful itself; we touch eternal life. From the liturgy, joy should radiate through the house; in it the problems of the day can again and again be transformed and overcome. When the liturgy is at the center of our life, the words of the Apostle apply to us: "Rejoice, again I say rejoice . . . the Lord is near" (Ph 4:4). It is only from the heart of the liturgy that we can understand what is meant when the Apostle Paul defines the priest of the New Covenant as "the servant of your joy" (2 Co 1:24).

When I was young, it was customary to think that preparation for the priesthood consisted essentially of learning to "read Mass". It was no wonder that this took so long, because it was also known that you had to learn Latin and that was no easy thing. With the right understanding it can really be said that in the ultimate analysis, preparation for the priesthood is concerned with learning to celebrate the Eucharist. The reverse, however, can also be said: the Eucharist is here in order to teach us about life. The school of the Eucharist is the school of right living; it leads us in just this way to the teaching of that which alone it can be said, I am the Way, the Truth, and the Life (Jn 14:6). The awesome aspect of the Eucharist lies in the fact that the priest may speak with the *I* of Christ. To become a priest and to be a priest involves a constant movement toward this identification. We are never finished with this, but if we are seeking it, then we are on the right path: on the path to God and man, on the pathway of love. This is the standard by which every formation for the priesthood must be gauged.

In closing, perhaps I may hazard a few thoughts concerning the application of these reflections to your symposium theme, "The Catholic Priest as Moral Teacher and Guide". I have said that the Eucharist is the center of preparation for the priesthood. Here we might say that Jesus, who is the Way, gives us himself, which is Truth and Life. One teaches truth. What are the implications of attempting to do otherwise? Can one possibly defend the teaching of something other than the truth? Some in our society may have so relativized their understanding of the word *truth* that it means something different for them than it does for us. But how can one defend the *teaching* of the communication of what one says makes sense only to oneself? If it makes sense only to me, I may think that way, but I have no right to teach it, which is to assert that it should mean something clear, something true, not just for oneself but for the other as well. And Jesus is also the Life. What can this mean for the priest, except that he must not merely teach; he must also live, act, behave in such a way that he can say, with the Apostle Paul, "It is now no longer I who live, but Christ who lives in me". Here we can see the great contours of the intimate unity between Truth and Life. I suspect this is what is meant when we affirm that the Priest is called to be both teacher and guide: he should teach only what is true, and what he teaches will be seen as a reliable guide for Christian life when the faithful see it lived out in the priest's own life.

Rev. Albert Vanhoye, S.J.

THE APOSTLE PAUL AS MORAL TEACHER AND GUIDE

INTRODUCTION

First of all, I would like to express my pleasure at being invited to participate in this symposium, which is a timely answer to the present need in the Church for an emphasis on moral theology. In particular, I am glad to have this opportunity to show the deep gratitude I feel toward His Eminence Cardinal Krol, a great friend and benefactor of the Gregorian Consortium, of which the Biblicum is one of three members.

As you know, I am not a specialist in moral theology but a Biblical scholar. I understand that the steering committee of the symposium has thought it useful to have a biblical point of view about moral teaching. Of course, my contribution cannot offer a complete view of the evolution of morality in the Bible. This would be a very complex subject. Nor can I explain the various points of view taken by the different authors of the New Testament—Matthew and John, Paul and James, and the others. I intend to limit myself to the presentation of only one author, but a very stimulating one, the Apostle Paul, who has introduced in the Church a new theological understanding of moral questions.

It is not easy to reach a correct understanding of Paul's teaching in those matters, because they are necessarily connected with the place that the Mosaic law has in Christian life. We shall nevertheless try to formulate the precise doctrinal position that Saint Paul has taken concerning the law, and then we shall examine the practical ways in which he teaches and guides the faithful in moral matters. Both of these areas are highly controversial. One current of opinion denies that either had a place in Paul's thought. Its proponents maintain that the Apostle had adopted a decidedly "antinomian" position, that he completely rejected the ancient *Nomos,* namely, the Mosaic law, and law of any sort. They say, correspondingly, that he never sought to impose any "binding precept" on his Christians but was satisfied to propose some suggestions to them, leaving them free to assent or to dissent. Other exegetes reject such an interpretation of Paul's moral theology as not faithful to the actual thinking of the Apostle and as contradicted by his practice. It is our task to cast some light on that question.

I. SAINT PAUL AND THE LAW

a. Saint Paul, an Antinomian

It is not difficult to assemble a series of Pauline texts to make Saint Paul appear antinomian—that is, systematically opposed to the Mosaic law. In the letter to the Galatians, the Apostle places a choice before Christians: either law or faith. This is an exclusive choice: who holds to the law rejects the faith; who accepts the faith denies the law. The problem Saint Paul poses there is that of "justification", a problem that is in itself juridical. The Bible does not make a clear distinction between moral matters and juridical domain. *To justify* expresses the action of a judge who, after an inquiry, declares that a person is justified, namely, that he has not infringed any law. Paradoxically, Saint Paul proclaims that the law does not serve to justify; that to conform one's actions to the law is useless, because, according to Saint Paul, no one can be justified before God by keeping the law. This declaration of Saint Paul is stated in the letter to the Galatians thus: "We acknowledge that a human being is not justified by works of the law, but by faith in Jesus Christ. Knowing that, we have become believers in Christ Jesus in order to be justified by faith in Christ and not by works of the law, because by works of the law *no one will be justified*" (Ga 2:15–16). This doctrine, a rather strange juridical viewpoint, is confirmed in the letter to the Romans, where Paul declares: "We hold that human beings are justified by faith, exclusive of works of the law" (Rm 3:28). In some of the following verses, Saint Paul does not hesitate to give a definition of God that is directly opposite to that of a just judge. The moral duty of a judge according to Deuteronomy 25:1 is "to justify the just and to condemn the impious"—that is, to "acquit the innocent and to condemn the guilty". In his prayer for the people, Solomon asks God to act in that manner (1 K 8:32) and, in fact, God declares in Exodus 23:7: "I will not justify the wicked". On the contrary, Saint Paul has the audacity to call God in Romans 4:5 "the one who justifies the impious", therefore attributing to God himself an attribute contrary to the law. It would be difficult to go further in antinomianism.

When Saint Paul describes the purpose of the law and its consequences, his expressions are extremely disparaging. "What then was the purpose of adding the law?" he asks in Galations 3:19, and answers: "This was done to specify crimes" (3:19). The letter to the Romans explains this too-concise reply, saying that, on the one hand, the law makes known the sin—"All that the law does is tell us what is sinful" (Rm 3:20)—and, on the other hand, the effect of the law is to provoke a multitude of sins—"When the law came, it was to multiply transgressions" (5:20). "Sin", he writes again, "took advantage of the commandment to mislead me, and so sin, through the commandment, killed me" (7:11). In this prospect, the law appears to be not only useless but, in spite of its good intentions, actually harmful.

As a result, according to Galatians 3:10, "Those who rely on the law are under a curse". Consequently, the work of Christ consists in "redeeming us from the curse of the law" (Ga 3:13). In fact, "[W]hen the appointed time came, God sent his Son, born of a woman, born a subject of the law, to redeem the subjects of the law" (Ga 4:4–5). Paul turns to the Galatians, who wanted "to be subject to the law" (Ga 4:21) and reproaches them vehemently, saying: "When Christ freed us, he meant for us to remain free. Stand firm, therefore, and do not submit again to the yoke of slavery" (Ga 5:1). Finally, Paul pronounces a formidable verdict: "If you look to the law to make you justified, then you have separated yourselves from Christ, and have fallen from grace" (Ga 5:4). On the contrary, in the letter to the Romans, Paul defines the authentic Christian position, saying: "[Y]ou are now under grace, not under the law" (Rm 6:14). If someone would say that these texts do not apply to every law, but only to the Mosaic law, one could reply that the arguments against the Mosaic law are even more valid against any other law, since Mosaic law has been considered more perfect than any other. If, then, the more perfect law is disqualified, so should *a fortiori,* other laws. It is therefore possible to find in Saint Paul's letters expressions of a strong antinomianism.

b. Saint Paul's Approval of the Law

Nevertheless, it is equally possible to find in the same letters the affirmation of a favorable attitude to the law. In the letter to the Galatians, the law appears to have a positive value when Saint Paul declares, "The whole law has found fulfillment in this one precept: "You shall love your neighbor as yourself" (Ga 5:14). Saint Paul again takes the same perspective in a more detailed manner in the letter to the Romans: "He who loves his neighbor has fulfilled the law. The commandments: you shall not commit adultery; you shall not murder; you shall not steal; you shall not covet, and any other commandment there may be, are all summed up in this: You shall love your neighbor as yourself. Love never does any wrong to the neighbor; hence, love is the fulfillment of the law" (Rm 13:8–10). It is clear in this text that Paul does not reject the commandments of the law. In chapter 7 of the letter to the Romans he declares openly that "the law is holy and the commandment is holy and just and good" (Rm 7:12); "We know", he says, "that the law is spiritual" (7:14); "I agree that the law is good" (7:16). In previous chapters, Paul has expressed the question "Are we then abolishing the law by means of faith?" (3:13). For one who has in mind Paul's polemics against the law in certain passages of the letter to the Galatians, the answer to that question must surely be affirmative: Paul abolishes the law by means of faith. The Apostle does not mean it like that, however. His answer is, "Not at all! We are confirming the law" (Rm 3:31). How true this is can be verified in Romans 8:4, when Saint Paul states the purpose of the Incarnation and the death of Christ in these terms: "so that *the just precept of the law might be fulfilled in us*" (8:4). The purpose of God, when he "sent his Son in the likeness of sinful flesh" (8:3), was to give us the ability to fulfill the just decisions of the law. This affirmation of Saint Paul attributes a high position to the law.

We therefore have two series of contrasting texts. With the first series, it is possible to present Paul as a radical antinomian; with the second series, one can present him as a resolute supporter of the law. An exegete who does not want to be one-sided must take account of both series and find an explanation for this strange coexistence, unless he rests satisfied, like Heikki Räisänen, with asserting that Paul is not consistent.[1]

c. An Explanation of the Contrast:
The Question of Foundation

A precise analysis and a methodical comparison can uncover an explanation.

It is necessary, above all, to take into account the Apostle's character. Saint Paul was a passionate and impulsive man. In polemics he often expresses himself in a one-sided and paradoxical

---

[1] On p. 228 of his book *Paul and the Law*, WUNT 29, (Tübingen: Mohr, 1983), Heikki Räisänen declares: "In sum, I am not able to find in the relevant literature *any* conception of the law which involves such inconsistencies or such arbitrariness as does Paul's."

manner, the better to insist upon the point that he has at heart.
Therefore, it is necessary to situate his affirmations and negations
in their proper contexts in order to evaluate their exact significance.

A second important point is that Paul, when speaking of the
law, has in mind various meanings that the word *torah* can have in
Hebrew. The fundamental meaning of *torah* is not "juridical
precept" but rather "instruction". To his people God gave certain
"instructions". The books of the Pentateuch that contain these
instructions and indicate their place in the context of the Exodus
story are called the Torah in Hebrew and the *Nomos* in Greek.
The word *nomos* or *law* can therefore designate, in some contexts
of Saint Paul's writings, the Pentateuch or even all of the Old
Testament: in other contexts it can designate the Mosaic legislation or any other legislation.

In some texts, Saint Paul clearly distinguishes the Torah as
divine revelation transmitted through the biblical stories from the
Torah as an institution that regulated the lives of the Israelites.
Saint Paul never questions the Torah as revelation, but he does
polemize against the Torah as institution. The two points of view
are joined in the sentence of Romans 3:21, "Now, the justice of
God has been manifested *apart from the law,* even though both law
and prophets *bear witness to it*—that justice of God which works
through faith in Jesus Christ for all who believe" (Rm 3:21). The
justice of God—that is, his initiative of redemption—has been
"witnessed by the law" inasmuch as the law—that is, the Sacred
Scripture—is the revelation of the plan of God; it has been fulfilled,
however, "independently of the law", inasmuch as the law is an
institution, because the redemption is transmitted by means of
faith and not by means of the Mosaic institution.

For the present symposium, the point that most interests us is
the Pauline quarrel with the law as an institution. What range
does it have? Is it also a dispute against the Mosaic law as a moral
teaching? Does it involve every moral teaching and every legal
institution?

The answer is that in his dispute, Paul struggles against a
certain religious pretension of the Mosaic law, first of all as a legal

institution, and also as a moral teaching. Further, such a dispute touches every kind of legal institution and moral teaching that would have a similar pretension. It is important, however, to observe that Saint Paul's viewpoint is a limited one. In Galatians and in the first chapters of Romans he is debating about the *basis* of justification. His struggle is about the *foundation* of the right relationship between human beings and God. Nothing less and nothing more. The Jews' conviction was that the right foundation consisted in accepting the law of the Covenant, by which acceptance the person was integrated into God's people. Among the Jewish Christians there arose a strong tendency to maintain this requirement in addition to faith in Christ. Therefore, those Jewish Christians, whom we call Judaizers, strove to force upon the gentile Christians the acceptance of the Mosaic law. Their point of view was not directly ethical, but religious and institutional. With his theological perspicacity Saint Paul recognized at once that such a position was incompatible with Christian faith and ruinous for the Christian apostolate. There cannot be two heterogeneous foundations for the right relationship with God, Christ on the one hand and a legal institution on the other. The only valid foundation is Christ. "If you look to the Law to make you justified, then you have separated yourselves from Christ and have fallen from grace" (Ga 5:4). Moreover, such a position was contrary to the universal dimension of Christ's redemptive work because it reduced the Church to a Jewish sect. Paul could not accept such a reduction; he used to instruct his pagan converts to "remain in the state" in which they were when called by God (1 Co 7:20). In his recent book on Paul's ethics, John M. G. Barclay rightly insists on the institutional point of view in Paul's dispute, a point of view that is neglected in the Lutheran interpretation of Paul's doctrine.[2]

We must admit, however, that the moral point of view is not absent. It is closely connected to the institutional one. Paul's

[2] John M. G. Barclay, *Obeying the Truth: A Study of Paul's Ethics in Galatians* (Edinburgh: T. & T. Clark, 1988), 240–41.

biblical education prevented him from separating the two completely. Paul was not only fighting against forcing acceptance of the Jewish way of life upon the gentiles. He was fighting at the same time against human pretense to base one's relationship with God on conformity of one's works to the law: "If I act according to the Law, I am just before God and God shall acknowledge that." Thinking like this, man makes everything depend on his own efforts, on his own accomplishments. This means he takes himself as a basis. Saint Paul resolutely rejects such an attitude because it carries a person to his perdition, fostering his pride and separating him from God. Nobody is capable of justifying himself or of saving himself. The only way to be justified is by receiving in faith the justification offered by God through Christ. At this fundamental level the law does not serve. The works are useless; the moral teaching has no place. Neither law nor moral teaching provides the basis of Christian life; the basis is grace, received by means of faith in Christ.

What Saint Paul says against the Mosaic law as moral teaching as well as legal institution is evidently valid against every moral teaching and every legal institution; such institutions must absolutely renounce the pretension of being the basis of Christian life.

But that does not mean that they have no place at all. Saint Paul refuses to give moral rules the position of foundation; he does not refuse to give them another position. On the contrary, Paul attributes great importance to Christian rules of morality. He does so, however, in a new perspective that deserves our full attention.

II. SAINT PAUL'S MORAL TEACHING AND PEDAGOGY

a. A Moral Teaching That Is Really Christian

What is new in the moral teaching of Saint Paul is that it is a morality founded on faith in Christ and in the dynamism of the Holy Spirit received through faith.

It is truly a morality; that is, it consists of rules to follow in order to avoid wrongdoing and to act rightly. Contrary to the opinion of Ernst Käsemann, who attributes to Paul a polemic attitude against good deeds ("polemic against all the good and pious works of men"),[3] it is clear that Paul never ceases to exhort his Christians to perform good deeds. Even in his letter to the Galatians, so much opposed to the pretensions of "the works of the law", Paul insists on the necessity of good works, saying,

> Do not be deceived; God is not mocked, for whatever a man sows, that he will also reap.... [L]et us not grow weary in *well-doing,* for in due season we shall reap, if we do not lose heart. So then, as we have opportunity, let us *do good* to all men, and especially to those who are of the household of Faith.
> (Ga 6:7, 9–10)

The apostle is never content to teach the faith; in every one of his letters he exhorts the believers to behave properly. In his letter to the Romans, for example, Paul's demand for good deeds is not delayed until the "moral section" (which begins in Chapter 12); but right in the heart of his great doctrinal statement, in Chapter 6, he inserts this vigorous exhortation: "Do not yield your members to sin as instruments of wickedness, but yield yourselves to God as men who have been brought from death to life, and your members to God as instruments of righteousness" (Rm 6:13). And a few verses later he repeats: "Just as you once yielded your members to impurity and to greater and greater iniquity, so now yield your members to righteousness for sanctification" (Rm 6:19). The good works, therefore, are indispensable, but they are no longer "works *of the law*", even if they correspond effectively to the demands of the law. The good works of the believers are works *of the Faith* — that is, works that have their origin in faith in Christ and that are accomplished with the help of the grace of

---

[3] Ernst Käsemann, "Ministry and Community in the New Testament", *Essays on New Testament Themes,* Studies in Biblical Theology 41 (London: SCM Press, 1964), 63–94.

God received by means of faith. Henceforth, "in Christ", what is important is "faith working through love" (*pistis di' agapēs energoumenē;* Ga 5:6).

Saint Paul is very attentive in his moral teaching not to restore the law to the place that he had denied it in his doctrinal teaching, that is, the position of foundation. In his letters he never exhorts Christians to observe the law, and this is easily understood, because "to observe the Law", we have shown, is an ambiguous expression. But one would expect, at least, that he would exhort Christians to observe the Decalogue, the Ten Commandments (cf. Mt 19:16–19 and parallels). The moral section of our catechisms is traditionally based on the Ten Commandments. One must note that this tradition has no basis in Saint Paul's manner of exhortation, at least as we have known it through his letters.

Saint Paul's moral teaching is not founded on the commandments, but on the relationship of the Christian with God through Christ in the Spirit. Already in the earliest of his letters he says to the neophytes, "You know what precepts we gave you *through the Lord Jesus*" (1 Th 4:2), and he relates the moral demands to the vocation received from God (4:7) and the gift of the Holy Spirit (4:8). The manner in which he treats the problem of the *porneia,* sexual immorality, in 1 Corinthians is particularly significant. Paul does not appeal to a commandment but to the relationship that one's body has with Christ and with the Spirit. "The body", he says, "is not meant for sexual immorality, but for the Lord, and the Lord for the body" (1 Co 6:13). Then he adds: "Do you not know that your bodies are members of Christ? Shall I therefore take the members of Christ and make them members of a prostitute?" That is really Christian moral teaching. The Apostle, however, does not despise anthropological considerations. He proposes one a little further on when he writes: "Every other sin which a man commits is outside the body; but the immoral man sins against his own body" (6:18). But he immediately jumps to a theological consideration: "Do you not know that your body is a temple of the Holy Spirit within you, which you have from God?" (6:19).

In a similar way, when he wants to eliminate the spirit of

rivalry that provokes divisions within the community, Paul appeals immediately to the relationship with Christ: "Is Christ divided?" he asks the Corinthians (1 Co 1:13). And to the Philippians he says: "Have this mind among yourselves, which you have in Christ Jesus, who, though he was in the form of God, did not count equality with God a thing to be grasped, but emptied himself, taking the form of a slave" (Ph 2:5–7). By these examples we can ascertain that some of the most profound doctrinal affirmations of Paul are contained in his moral teaching. This fact shows to what extent his moral teaching is truly Christian.

b. Did Paul Impose "Binding Precepts"?

From the Pauline polemics against the law certain authors have concluded that, according to the Apostle, "[T]he Christian is no longer liable to the claim of particular precepts." In his book about the pastoral anthropology of Saint Paul, Father Jerome Murphy-O'Connor proclaims that there are "no binding precepts" in the moral teaching of Saint Paul.[4] Paul "refused to consider the directives of the Law and of Jesus as precepts", and *a fortiori* he did not "intend his own directives to impose a binding obligation".[5] Fr. Murphy-O'Connor had previously explained his thesis in another book published in French.[6] In his opinion, binding precepts are incompatible with a free and authentic existence; therefore, it is unthinkable that the Apostle could enjoin precepts of such a kind on Christians, who are called to freedom (cf Ga 5·1).

In a doctoral dissertation defended at the Biblicum, Fr. T. J. Deidun has convincingly refuted Fr. Murphy-O'Connor's opin-

---

[4] Jerome Murphy-O'Connor, O.P., *Becoming Human Together: The Pastoral Anthropology of St. Paul,* Good News Studies 2 (Wilmington, Del.: Glazier, 1982), 199.

[5] Murphy-O'Connor, *Becoming Human Together,* 202.

[6] Jerome Murphy-O'Connor, O.P., *L'existence chrétienne selon saint Paul,* Lectio Divina 80 (Paris: Cerf, 1974).

ion by means of a thorough study of Pauline texts.[7] Even from a philosophical point of view the thesis that binding precepts are incompatible with a free and authentic existence is far from being beyond question; rather, we must acknowledge that binding precepts and freedom are reciprocally related. However that may be, it is certain that Paul enjoined binding precepts energetically. Fr. Deidun has demonstrated, for instance, the force of the Pauline injunction, in 1 Thessalonians 4:3, to "abstain from sexual immorality". In that passage Paul specifies that "this is the will of God" (4:3) and that nonobservance of this point (1) contradicts the Christian's vocation (4:7), (2) constitutes resistance to God's own saving activity in us (4:8), and (3) incurs eschatological punishment (4:6b).[8] One can wonder what more is needed to render binding any precept.

In 1 Corinthians, Paul makes a clear distinction between a simple advice (*gnōmēn didōmi;* 1 Co 7:25) and a "command of the Lord" (*epitagēn Kyriou;* 1 Co 7:25). The command of the Lord, expressed in verse 10, is that the wife should not separate from her husband nor the husband dismiss his wife.

Saint Paul recalls several times the binding negative precepts he used to teach. Instead of presenting them as precepts of the law, he presented them as requirements absolutely necessary to *"inherit the kingdom of God"*. A similar perspective is to be found in the Gospel story of the rich young man: "What must I do to *inherit* eternal life? . . . How hard it is to enter *the kingdom of God!*" (Macc 10:17, 23; Lk 18:18, 24), but in the Gospels Jesus quotes the Decalogue. Paul does not. He writes to the Galatians:

> The works of the flesh are plain: immorality, impurity, licentiousness; idolatry, sorcery; enmity, strife, jealousy, anger, selfishness, dissension, party spirit, envy; drunkenness, carousing, and the like. *I warn you, as I warned you before,* that *those who do such things shall not inherit the kingdom of God.*
>
> (Ga 5:19–21)

---

[7] T. J. Deidun, *New Covenant Morality in Paul,* An. Bibl. 89 (Rome: P.I.B., 1981); see pt. IV, "Love and Law in New Testament Morality", 150–226.

[8] T. J. Deidun, "Love and Law", 182.

The words "as I warned you before" clearly show that Paul had included this binding moral teaching in his previous cathechesis. In I Corinthians we find a similar list, except that instead of names of vices Paul uses names of vicious men: "Neither the immoral, nor idolaters, nor adulterers, nor homosexuals, nor thieves, nor the greedy, nor drunkards, nor revilers, nor robbers will inherit the kingdom of God" (I Co 6:9–10). The same moral teaching is also repeated in Ephesians 5:5.[9]

In addition to this general moral teaching, Paul could give precise orders to put an end to any abnormal situation. He claimed that Christ had given him authority to do so and that he could be severe in using that "authority" (*exousia;* 2 Co 10:8, 13:10). To the Corinthians he asks: "What do you wish? Shall I come to you *with a rod?*" (I Co 4:21). Another time, he threatens them: "I warned those who sinned before and all the others and *I warn them now* while absent . . . that if I come again *I will not spare them*" (2 Co 13:2). Obviously, his desire was that the warning would suffice. "I write this", he explains, "while I am away from you, in order that when I come I may not have to be severe" (2 Co 13:10). In some cases, he did not hesitate to take rigorous measures — for instance, against the man who was "living with his father's wife". He decided that this man was to be "handed over to Satan" and thus exposed to every kind of physical disease, with the hope that "his spirit may be saved in the day of the Lord Jesus" (I Co 5:1–5). To the charismatics in Corinth, Paul gave very strict rules of behavior in the Christian assembly (I Co 14:27–30) and presented these rules as a "command of the Lord" (14:37). In that matter he permitted no dissent.

---

[9] The direct Pauline authenticity of Ephesians is dubious. Many consider it "Deutero-pauline". Ep 5:5 has the particular phrase "the kingdom of the Christ and of God" (cf. Rv 11:15).

c. Paul's Moral Pedagogy

We must therefore maintain that there are indeed "binding precepts" in the moral teaching of Saint Paul, both general ones and particular ones. But it is important to acknowledge, at the same time, that those binding precepts did not constitute the main part of Saint Paul's moral theology and pedagogy. Whereas the Decalogue consists almost exclusively of prohibitions ("You shall have no other gods before me; you shall not make a graven image . . . ; you shall not kill; you shall not commit adultery" and so forth), Saint Paul's moral teaching is chiefly positive, dynamic, inventive.

The principal preoccupation of the Apostle was not to insist on the limitations to be respected in order to avoid sin and God's punishment, but rather to *encourage in every way the development of the new life* received through faith and baptism (cf. Rm 6:4). Saint Paul was deeply convinced of the strength of that new life, the strength of the Holy Spirit, who dwells in Christians (cf. 1 Co 3:16, 6:19; Rm 8:9) and pours into their hearts all the dynamism of the divine *agapē* (Rm 5:5). For that reason, Saint Paul constantly invites the faithful to go ahead, to make progress, literally to "abound" (*perisseuein*). He praises the Thessalonians because they are doing as he has taught them, and at the same time exhorts them to "abound", to do so more and more (1 Th 4:1). After that general exhortation, he specifies some points: "Concerning love of the brethren", he declares, "you have no need to have any one write to you, for you yourselves have been taught by God to love one another and indeed you do love all the brethren throughout Macedonia". Nevertheless, he exhorts them to "abound", to do so more and more (1 Th 4:9–10). Writing to the Galatians, he urges them to "walk by the Spirit" (Ga 5:16), that is, to behave according to the dynamism of the Holy Spirit. "If we live by the Spirit", he adds, "let us also walk by the Spirit" (Ga 5:25).

Saint Paul knew that the most secure way of avoiding sin is not to be preoccupied in avoiding it, but rather to invest all one's efforts in doing good. "Walk by the Spirit", he writes, "and you will not be in danger of gratifying the desires of the flesh" (Ga

5:16). Usually, the second part of this sentence is not well understood. The Revised Standard Version translates it with an imperative—"[D]o *not gratify* the desires of the flesh"; the Greek text, however, has no imperative in this place but instead a reinforced negative assertion (*ou mē* with subjunctive). The meaning is clear. Paul inculcates a dynamic attitude as the best way to be preserved from sin. His reason is not simply a psychological one but chiefly theological: the Spirit, which dwells in the Christian, is stronger than the flesh. Hence the Christian is called to rely on the strength of the Spirit instead of remaining preoccupied with the necessity of defending himself against possible temptations. Such depressing preoccupation is rather harmful because it usually aggravates the danger. The dynamic attitude is the correct one, on the condition that it not be founded on human presumption but on docility to God's grace.

Saint Paul observes that the Christian who welcomes in his own life the dynamism of the divine love activated by the Holy Spirit will then, without even thinking of it, fulfill every commandment of the law and actually go beyond it. "He who loves his neighbor has fulfilled the law. . . . Love does no wrong to a neighbor; therefore love is the fulfilling of the law" (Rm 13:8, 10). Docility to the Holy Spirit places the Christian on a morally higher level than do the requirements of the law. In fact, "the fruit of the Spirit is love, joy, peace, patience, kindness, goodness, faithfulness, gentleness, self-control", and "against such there is no law" (Ga 5:22–23). For that reason, Saint Paul does not hesitate to declare: "If you are led by the Spirit, you are not under the law" (Ga 5:18); "You are not under the law but under grace" (Rm 6:14). It is evident that, on that level, there is no more place for "binding precepts". The binding precepts indicate the level below which the Christian may not go without grave infidelity to his vocation. If he transgresses them, he separates himself from God's grace and loses his Christian freedom, becoming "a slave to sin" (Jn 8:34). But while he lives in docility to the Spirit, he finds himself in a region of authentic freedom, where his behavior is not predetermined.

Saint Paul invites the Christian to be *inventive* in his moral life instead of submitting himself to worldly conformism. "Do not be conformed to this world", he says, "but be transformed by the renewal of your mind, that you may discern (*dokimazein*) what is the will of God, what is good and acceptable and perfect" (Rm 12:2). Saint Paul thinks of the will of God, not as a prefabricated rule already fixed in the written law, but as a creative reality, which is to be discovered in its continually renewed dynamism. The condition making that discovery possible is not an intellectual capacity but a spiritual one, which Paul expresses when he writes to the Philippians: "It is my prayer that your love may abound more and more with knowledge and all insight, so that you may discern (*dokimazein*) what is excellent" (Ph 1:10). Progress in love is the main condition for a moral discernment.

In saying this, Saint Paul proposes a very positive appreciation of God's will. Far from being only an object of fear or of resignation, God's will is thought of as a treasure to be discovered and a source of life and joy.

Another aspect of Saint Paul's moral pedagogy is the care he takes to give *detailed explanations.* He does not rest satisfied with simply imposing precepts or decisions, but he endeavors to make the reasons for them understood, so as to obtain from his Christians a really human assent and a willing obedience. This is particularly manifest in 1 Corinthians, where he treats at length several moral problems, such as divisions in the Christian community, sexual behavior, the question of eating food consecrated to pagan gods, the problem of charisms and so forth. He patiently considers them from different points of view; shows their relationships to Christology, to ecclesiology; uses examples taken from his own experience and so helps the faithful better understand what they must do and how they must do it, in the light of the Christian faith and under the impulse of Christian love.

Last but far from least, Saint Paul reinforced his teaching with the *example of his own behavior.* He was extremely conscious of the necessity of doing this. For instance, when he writes 1 Thessalonians, instead of presenting a code of precepts, he recalls the example that he has given—"[Y]ou are witness, and God also, how holy and righteous and blameless was our behavior to you" (1 Th 2:10)—and he congratulates the faithful because, he says, "you became imitators of us" (1 Th 1:6). In other letters, Saint Paul directly exhorts Christians to follow his examples: "I urge you, then, be imitators of me" (1 Co 4:16). "Be imitators of me, my brothers. Take as your guide those who follow the example that we set" (Ph 3:17). "Live according to . . . what you have heard me say and seen me do. Then will the God of peace be with you" (Ph 4:9). This kind of exhortation corresponds to Paul's temperament; he had a clear propensity to putting himself forward and speaking about himself. A more modest temperament would not express itself in the same way. It remains true, however, that the concern to be a model for the faithful constitutes an indispensable part of the pastoral ministry, as we can see in 1 Peter, where it is placed in contrast to the spirit of domination (1 P 5:3). Saint Paul took this most seriously. In order to "give in his conduct an example to imitate" (2 Th 3:9),[10] he even renounced the apostolic right to live at the expense of the community and chose to "work with his own hands" (1 Co 4:12; 1 Th 2:9). Thus he could write to the faithful, "You yourselves know how you ought to imitate us; we were not idle when we were with you; we did not eat any one's bread without paying, but with toil and labor we worked night and day" (2 Th 3:7–8). Evidently, the ultimate rule for Christian behavior is not the apostle, but the Lord; Saint Paul was fully conscious of that and therefore completed his exhortation, "Be imitators of me, *as I am of Christ*" (1 Co 11:1; cf. 1 Th 1:6). In that way, his moral teaching and pedagogy reach their perfection.

---

[10] The Pauline authenticity of 2 Th is matter of dispute among modern exegetes; however, excellent experts such as B. Rigaux and W. Kümmel consider the arguments opposed to the authenticity as not decisive. They need not prevail against the ancient testimonies unanimously favorable to the authenticity.

CONCLUSION

For the "Catholic priest as moral teacher and guide" the Apostle Paul is certainly a most illuminating and stimulating character; not because a complete treatise of ethics could be found in his letters, but because Paul traced the fundamental orientations of an authentically Christian moral *theology*. Saint Paul made it clear that the basis for such a moral theology could not be the law, neither the Jewish Torah nor any other legal system. The basis must be Christ and the personal relationship with him through faith. The basis is Christ's life in every one of us. "It is not longer I who live, but Christ who lives in me" (Ga 2:20).

Christ's life in us requires the observance of certain moral precepts. Far from being removed from us, such binding precepts become more obligatory because they determine the level below which Christ's life in us would be suffocated by our own fault. But Christian life does not properly consist in observing those moral precepts, no more than a mother's love consists in not killing her own child. Christian life consists in doing much better than the requirements of the precepts, in freedom, under the impulse of the Holy Spirit. By emphasizing that point Saint Paul introduced a new understanding of morality — a positive, dynamic, inventive one. I am not sure that the usual way of teaching morality in the Church has been faithful enough to that new understanding. If I am not wrong, there has been a tendency to confound two domains that should be distinguished: the domain of the binding precepts and that of the positive Christian life. This tendency considers everything only from the point of view of moral obligation. The result is that Christian life may appear as a new legal system, more meticulous than any other, and therefore not attractive. It would be doctrinally more exact and pastorally more fruitful to distinguish the two domains and to include both in the moral teaching, with a particular emphasis on the second one, the domain of spiritual inventiveness, which is more specific to Christian life.

A RESPONSE TO
REV. ALBERT VANHOYE, S.J.

by Rev. Msgr. James J. Mulligan, S.T.D.

Father Vanhoye spoke of the newness of Saint Paul's understanding of morality. He concluded that the teaching of morality in the Church has, perhaps, not been faithful enough to that new understanding. Confusing the domain of binding precept with the domain of positive Christian life gives the appearance of a new legal system, more meticulous than any other, and is therefore not attractive. I find myself in full agreement with his position.

The theme of this symposium is "The Catholic Priest as Moral Teacher and Guide". In this response I would like to suggest some ways in which we can give new life to the teaching of moral theology by paying more attention to the depth of what Saint Paul wrote in his epistles. There are three points in particular that can help us: (1) Saint Paul's awareness of the entrance into a new life in Christ, (2) the need to refer, as Paul always does, to the living experience that we all share, and (3) a deeper awareness of what sin actually is.

NEW LIFE IN CHRIST

In the First Epistle to the Corinthians Paul first develops his magnificent theme of the Body of Christ. I think that we too easily fall into the trap of speaking of this as though it means simply our unity in the Church, the Mystical Body of Christ. Actually, he means much more than that. To enter into unity with the Body of Christ is not simply to enter into a community; it is to enter into a living union with Christ himself.

Paul ultimately describes this union in terms that are unmistakably trinitarian: "No one understands the thoughts of God but the

Spirit of God. But the Spirit that we have received is not that of the world, but the Spirit that comes from God" (1 Co 2:11–12). It is by reason of this Spirit that everything we do or say has a dimension that it would not otherwise have. We are no longer men of the flesh (*sarkikos*). We are no longer ruled by sin and mortality. We are no longer simply bodily (*somatikos*), living only as part of this material world. We are no longer simply men moved by our own human power to know and to love (*psychikos*). Instead, we are spiritual beings (*pneumatikos*), capable of knowing and loving in union with the knowledge and love of God himself. "The spiritual man is alive to all true values, but his own true value no unspiritual man can see. For who has ever known the Lord's thoughts, so that he can instruct him? But we share the thoughts of Christ!" (1 Co 2:15–16). To know and love in union with the knowledge and love of God is to enter into his own life. It is to be one with the Son who is the Word of God and one with the Spirit who is the love of God. It is in this union that we are able, finally, to relate to the Father.

EXPERIENCE

All too often, this consciousness of trinitarian life forms part of our dogma but not a clear enough part of our morality. This is precisely what Paul always seems to have so clearly in mind: to live a life of Christian morality is not a matter of human acquiescence to a moral law; it is, rather, to live to its depths a new life and a new wisdom "hitherto kept secret, and destined by God before the world began for our glory" (1 Co 2:7).

Paul does not present this simply as a doctrine that demands an intellectual assent of faith. Instead, it is a reality that we can identify in our own experience if we only take the trouble to look. "For you have grown rich in everything through union with him — in power of expression and in capacity for knowledge. So your *experience* has confirmed the testimony that I bore to

Christ" (1 Co 1:5–6). "Consider, brothers, what happened when God called you. Not many of you were what men call wise, not many of you were influential, not many were of high birth. . . . But you are his children through your union with Christ" (1 Co 1:26–30).

We do not, I think, often enough appeal to experience. We need to bring people to face in themselves what they are like when they live this new life in Christ, and what they are like when they do not. We need to identify that experience in ourselves and use that knowledge for others. Paul never hesitated to do so. When he spoke of his own behavior as "holy and righteous and blameless" (1 Th 2:10), it was so that he could call the Thessalonians to experience the same thing. He called others to be imitators of him (cf. 1 Th 1:6; Ph 3:17), not as if he were promoting himself but so that they could then also know within themselves what he was saying. "Live according to . . . what you have heard me say and seen me do. Then will the God of peace be with you" (Ph 4:9).

He even reminds the Corinthians that his own weakness was a sign that God's power had worked through him at the time of their conversion. He had come from Athens to Corinth tired, dejected and sick.

> So when I came to you, brothers, I did not come and tell you the secret purpose of God in superior, philosophical language, for I resolved, while I was with you, to forget everything but Jesus Christ and his crucifixion. For my part, I came among you in weakness and with a great deal of fear and trembling, and my teaching and message were not put in plausible, philosophical language, but they were attended with convincing spiritual power, so that your faith might rest, not on human philosophy, but on the power of God.
>
> (1 Co 2:1–5)

THE REALITY OF SIN

Sin is not simply the violation of a rule. It is the destroyer of the new life. It is the cause of pain and death. It undermines the very reality of what we are. It turns light into darkness and wisdom into foolishness (cf. Rm 1:18–32).

Here, too, our own experience can teach us, but perhaps it fails to do so partly because we are so used to an image that fails to convey the reality of sin. We tend to look at morality as a series of rules, with punishments attached to their violation—somewhat like traffic laws. We are told to stay within a certain speed limit, but the limit is rather arbitrary and, unless we are caught or have an accident, there is likely to be no punishment.

A far better image might be to compare moral laws to labels on bottles of poison. When we violate a rule such as "Thou shalt not speed", we may experience almost no bad effects. But when we violate a rule such as "Thou shalt not use internally", we get sick or die. When I choose to steal something from you, I am not only saying that you are not worth my consideration. I am also beginning to imply that you too can steal from me, and so I begin to undermine even myself. When I kill someone, not only do I take his life, but also I begin to imply that human life (my own included) is worth nothing. Every sin has this same self-destructive quality about it. And every sinner feels the pain.

One of our jobs in the teaching of morality is to help people identify their experience of the newness of life in Christ and the depth of pain that comes from sin. Sin is not the violation of a rule. It is the imbibing of a poison that slowly degrades and finally kills.

If we are to be effective as teachers of morality, then we must begin with ourselves and our own experience. We must begin to see the difference between a life lived in full union with Christ and a life lived in the shadow of sin and death. We must not be satisfied with formulating and teaching clear statements of principle. Rather, we must live with our hearts as well as our heads. We must both live and teach the real *experience* of the love of God as it has come to us in our life in the Trinity.

Rev. Georges Chantraine, S.J.

THE PRIEST IN THE SERVICE OF LIFE IN CHRIST ACCORDING TO THE LAW OF THE CHURCH

INTRODUCTION

The title of my paper demands a brief explanation. By "the priest", I mean he who receives the power of orders, the bishop and the priest. What I say will also apply to the deacon to some extent.

Priestly service flows from a mission received by ordination to the priesthood; consequently, it is not simply a function but a *commitment of the person.* The object of this commitment is to help one's brothers live more fully in Christ according to the law of the Spirit. This commitment is, in effect, to be at the service of their baptismal grace nourished by the Eucharist. Such a life is guided and animated by the law of the Spirit; neither a natural morality nor a morality of commandments suffice, for they are not the law of the *Spirit.* Not even enthusiasm and conscience suffice, even if they are spiritual, without the *law* that also belongs to the Spirit of Christ.

For a better understanding of the priest's mission and ministry, it will be good to recall the mystery of Christ that joins them together. After this discussion, we will examine the objective and subjective poles of priestly service, its diverse tasks and the spheres in which it is exercised.

I. THE EVENT OF CHRIST

The Christ contemplated by the author of the Epistle to the Hebrews is the Son of God and High Priest according to the order of Melchizedeck. It is about his sitting at the right hand of the divine majesty that the Father declares, "You are my Son, this day I have begotten you"; and about where the High Priest is enthroned, "Sit on my right. You are a priest according to the order of Melchizedek" (Ps 110:4). Christ *is* the Son from all eternity, he who is "the reflection of the glory and the image of the divine substance ... by whom God created all things"; he *became* High Priest, he whom God established as his "heir" "at the end of time" by the offering he once and for all made of his life, which he received from the Father. From all eternity he receives that which he is—his being as Son—and offers it to the Father in thanksgiving in the Spirit, whom he shares with the Father and who is distinct from each. In "his days in the flesh", he likewise received from his Father what he is in his Body, which God "created" for him (Heb 10:5), and offered it to the Father in the Holy Spirit, "tasting death for all men by the grace of God". The author of the epistle thus contemplates the coincidence of the eternal sonship and of the priesthood already accomplished in Christ sitting at the right hand. Saint Thomas Aquinas offers the same contemplation when he shows that the order of missions follows the order of processions. The priesthood is the mission of the Son; it transposes and adequately expresses in "economy", in human history, the relationship of the Father and Son. Therefore, in the priestly act one contemplates and receives the filial act itself.

Sonship and priesthood are thus linked together. In their scriptural commentaries the Fathers of the Church kept this connection in view, yet it seems to have received scant attention from modern theologians. A Dominican, Sister Marie de la Trinité, was placed by a particular grace *in sinu Patris,* where the Son springs forth and where the priesthood springs forth as well. Her charism, destined for the benefit of all (1 Co 12:7), is capable of reactivating an essential doctrine of Revelation. We will gradually see how.

Because in "the will" of God "we have been sanctified through the offering of the body of Jesus Christ once for all" (Heb 10:10) and through "one offering he has made perfect forever those who are sanctified" (Heb 10:14), share in the priesthood of the Son and thus in the sonship for which God the Father destined them (Heb 2:10). Because he is sanctified, the Christian shares in the priesthood and sonship of Christ. This participation of the baptized in the sonship and priesthood of Christ is not just the result of the offering of Christ, as the author of the Epistle to the Hebrews shows; it was willed by Christ, as Saint John shows in his Gospel. In pointing to John, Jesus on the Cross says in effect to his mother, "Woman, behold your son"; and to John, "Behold, your mother" (Jn 19:26). To the woman, personal symbol of the Church, with whom he unites himself, he gives himself with the fruit that is identically himself in John: John is Jesus and Mary is the mother of John, who takes her into his home. Like the companion whom God gives to man and whom the creating Word himself gives on the Cross, the Woman—that is, Mary—receives the fruitfulness that accomplishes the salvation of humankind. Mary participates in a feminine manner in the priesthood and in the sonship of Christ in giving to John the possibility of becoming son. She exercises the royal priesthood, which in her case is eminently personal.

Thus sonship and priesthood are joined in Christ Jesus and in Mary, the personal symbol of the Church. With John, every believer is a son of God by being born of the incarnate Word and of the Woman, the marian Church, and so is capable of exercising the royal priesthood. Mary-Church first receives this priesthood with her maternity. And because Saint John and the author of the Epistle to the Hebrews—like the great Tradition—unite creation and redemption, it is proper to say that the Christian acquires the fullness of his created being, which is to be son and thus person, precisely in becoming a priest in Christ, and also by accomplishing his priestly mission according to the directions that the Spirit gives to him. To the extent one joins sonship and priesthood in the Christian, one will speak, with Marie de la Trinité, followed by Hans Urs von Balthasar, of the "common priesthood of the faithful"[1] as well as of a "personal priesthood". The two expressions are not exclusive. The first designates the sacramental origin of the priesthood, "the regeneration and the anointing of the Holy Spirit".[2] The second emphasizes the effect of the sacrament, or the *res sacramenti:* the baptized exercises the priesthood as a son of God; the priesthood is a mission; it is given to a person and gives him the ability to realize himself as a person.[3] Saint John shows this in Mary and John at the foot of the Cross of Jesus. Viewing the priesthood from these perspectives, one better sees that the priesthood is not primarily an office—a *munus*—but a mission given by the Son, the Man perfect in his offering, to the Church, his Bride; and by her to each of her children. The priesthood is therefore personal in being ecclesial and in preserving in itself the feminine figure of the Church. In the personal priesthood of the Christian, the union with Christ includes a face-to-face relationship similar to that between a man and his wife; it is an interior nuptial union similar to the union of God and his people. If one accepts the consideration of the feminine, marian, and ecclesial quality of the personal priesthood of the faithful, one will more justly and openly situate the demands and certain claims of feminism. It seems imprudent and perhaps practically impossible to understand the ministry of the priest by abstracting from such a consideration. This further requires the joining of (1) sonship and priesthood, (2) person and mission, (3) the incarnate Word and Mary-Church as Bridegroom and Bride, and (4) the believing person and the Church.

Jesus anticipated the gift of himself, offered on the Cross, at the Last Supper by entrusting it to his Church in the hands of his

---

[1] LG 10.

[2] Ibid.

[3] This reality—the *res sacramenti*—was truly considered neither by *Lumen Gentium* nor by the last synod concerning the vocation and mission of the laity. It merits being in the line of Vatican II and of the development of its doctrine.

disciples, whom he had chosen to be with him and to exercise his ministry with his own power. It is to them that he gave the order "Do this in memory of me." The ancient memorial of the Passover became that of the paschal sacrifice of the Lord. The apostles received the order and thus the power to celebrate it in the name of the Lord. Mary did not receive this order nor this power; by *power* I mean that which makes one capable of carrying out the order, of celebrating the memorial of the Lord in his name. This of course does not mean that the faithful are not capable of offering themselves in offering the Lord, but only that this ever-new capability is theirs from the memorial of the Lord made present *hic et nunc* by those whom the Lord appointed to this office and by all those who, by the will of the apostles, have succeeded them. The Apostle John took Mary his mother into his home, that is to say, into his apostolic ministry, which came to him directly from the Lord and which is made fruitful by Mary-Church. In John, the apostolic Church is joined to the marian Church, she receives from the marian Church her fruitfulness, and she is distinct from Mary-Church. With Peter as her head, she is in the service of sinners, who are all those to be evangelized and who remain in a certain way converted to God. Made up of sinners, she offers them the forgiveness of God in the words of reconciliation, in the Eucharist of the Lord and in the other sacraments, in a communal life governed by charity. While the marian Church is without stain or wrinkle, those who are sinners have the command to manifest in the community of brothers the presence of the Lord, head and leader of the community, and his vivifying action even in the deadly acts committed by the brothers and sisters living with them in the world. This command surpasses human strength: Who can represent the Lord as head of his Church, as leader and shepherd of the community? The answer comes from the Lord: it is neither his Mother nor any of his sons through the gift of his grace. It is they whom he himself chose and sent, and among whom, he knows, is a traitor, Judas, and a renegade, Peter—and it is the latter whom Jesus chose to be Peter, the rock on which he built his Church. The apostolic Church thus plunges into the depths of sin where the Son descended to save us. She shows us the disfigured face of the Lord. Yet this humbled Jesus is the vivifying Lord. This is my Body given up; this is my Blood poured out.

Such a configuration of the glorified Christ who remains in his Church as the Suffering Servant is a grace conferred by the Lord himself on his apostles at the Last Supper. Just as Paul, with the presbyters, conferred it on Timothy by the imposition of hands, so the bishops, successors of Timothy and the other collaborators of the apostles, have transmitted it to their successors: it is the grace of the sacrament of orders. It is the grace of a service, for he who receives it is placed by the Lord in the service of his brothers to make the Lord present among them. So this service is filled with grace: it is the service of a believer who has received the mission to manifest in himself the Lord, leader and shepherd of the community. Because it is the grace of a service, the priesthood is ministerial, not personal; because this service is filled with grace, it is "charismatic". For the first reason, the dignity of the minister does not condition the service of grace: whether the priest is in the state of grace or not, Mass is validly celebrated and absolution is validly conferred. For the second reason, the priestly grace produces the holiness of the ministry and so builds up the Church. These are the objective and subjective poles about which I will speak. Before I proceed to this second part, however, it is good to consider just how far the gift of the Lord to men in the ministerial priesthood goes.

None of the caricatures that the world has presented of the pope, bishops and priests exceeds the figure of the humiliated Christ. If one thought that a particular caricature did exceed it—for example, the Roman claim to control the Church—one would make of her a counter-figure or a satanic image; one would desire to purify the Church and her faith, but would be tearing it away from the Church. It is the mystery of the Cross that one would no longer see in her: one would no longer look upon him whom they have pierced. Despite his theology of the Cross, Luther did not resist this temptation, and I fear that, for other reasons and without the theological and spiritual genius of the reformer, Archbishop Lefebvre also yielded to it. After the reformer, to the good and healthy anti-clericalism that criticizes the abuses of the priesthood and its power was added another criticism, one that takes aim at the ministerial priesthood or the hierarchical Church precisely at the point where the humiliation and the glory of the Lord are united: how this mystery of humiliation and glorification could be represented by a historical institution is what is not understood by the thought emanating from the Enlightenment, notably from Hegel and Nietzsche. For this reason, it is important to join the personal priesthood and the ministerial priesthood, sonship and priesthood, person and mission, incarnate Word and Mary-Church, person and Church, not only in consideration of reality, but also in consideration of the thought that issued from the Reformation and from the Enlightenment.

2. OBJECTIVE AND SUBJECTIVE POLES OF PRIESTLY MINISTRY

Ministry is holy and the source of holiness, for it flows from priestly grace: it is conferred on a person who is invested with it, and it is destined for persons. These are the two poles of priestly ministry: the objective and the subjective. The tension between the two poles defines the nature of the service conferred by the Lord to his priests.

Ministry is holy. The bishop is the visible source and foundation of his Church; he makes present in his person Christ the Lord, who is the leader and shepherd of the Church. The priests whom he puts in charge of communities in the diocese likewise make present the same Lord in their obedience to the bishop. Bishops and priests act in their ministry *in persona Christi Capitis.* Of course, every Christian is configured to Christ by his baptism: *christianus alter Christus.* Yet only those who have the grace of the priesthood have the capability of manifesting Christ, the Head of his Church and image of the Father, in the midst of his own. The Lord is, in effect, Head of the Church, his Bride, inasmuch as he possesses manhood in himself and he is, as Son, the image of the Father from whom he and all good things proceed (Jn 1:17). Because they represent Christ, Head of the Church and image of the Father, bishops and priests are enabled to make of the meeting of the brothers an assembly called together by God, of their *congregatio,* a *convocatio.* Here there are two dimensions of the Church: one is horizontal—that is, the meeting, the congregation of brothers who share the same faith and who manifest it to one another by the celebration of the sacraments and by fraternal charity; the other is vertical—that is, the *convocatio,* the coming in response to God, who calls his people together and who makes them his people, different from the world, to send them into the world, among men to save men. According to the first dimension, life becomes fraternal; what joins the members of the *congregatio* is not their belonging to a social class, a neighborhood, a region, a country, a continent, or a co-option by way of tastes, interests and so forth, but their freely chosen communal belonging to Jesus Christ. They are brothers in Jesus Christ because God the Father freely chose them in his Son and loves them through the Crucified One in the power of the Spirit. The convocation is the act by which this eternal choice and this trinitarian love are made visible and are effectively inscribed in the history of these men as the history of the Son who died for them and is seated at the right hand of the Father, living forever to intercede on their behalf. Bishops and priests have the task of convoking men in the name of God the Father and of his Son, interceding for them in the power of the Spirit, in view of making them sons who will become brothers to one another with "the firstborn among many brothers" (Rm 8:29). This is why bishops and priests act *in persona Christi Capitis.* Their ministry is, in the first place, a mission; it is so in a double sense: they are themselves sent among men to bring men to God, to worship him, to praise him, to adore him, and to serve him; and they have the office of sending on the mission their brothers thus convoked, not in their own names but in the name of the Lord. Thus each person is sent directly by the Lord; and the mission of each, in what is useful for all, stems from the discernment of the pastor, be he bishop or priest. The pastoral plan gives form to the missions of each person: it does not substitute itself for the Holy Spirit or for each of the brothers; it is at the service of the Christian life and of missionary growth, which comes at the same time from the Holy Spirit and the generosity of Christian hearts. It is so through the *paraclesis,* that is to say, both exhortation and consolation (see Saint Paul, Balthasar), through the discernment of gifts and by the vigilance of fraternal charity.

Since Vatican II, the development of the ecclesiastical bureaucracy has paralleled that of states, employing too many priests who have become unfit for their ministries or who spend almost all their time making reports on meetings: the offices of episcopates or of bishops' conferences have multiplied projects said to be pastoral, to the elaboration of which the faithful are sometimes associated, as in the case in the United States. Because of these practices and others, the idea of a pastoral plan and pastoral ministry has itself changed. Without realizing it, some bishops and priests have been transformed into administrators. This analysis does not seem off the mark.

At the time of the 1987 synod on the vocation and mission of the laity, I observed a good number of bishops reserving to themselves the initiative and organization of the pastoral plan, requiring Christians to cooperate with what they had decided to do. They do not take well to initiatives that elude their control. The crystallizing point can be found in their relations with lay movements. They forget canon 215, of which it has been necessary to remind them:

> The Christian faithful are at liberty freely to found and to govern associations for charitable and religious purposes or for the promotion of the Christian vocation in the world; they are free to hold meetings to pursue these purposes in common.

Such freedom is understood by a pastor who is himself free. For priestly freedom consists in configuration to Christ the Head and is exercised in the act of convoking men and sending them in the name of God to announce salvation through Jesus Christ. The more a bishop or priest is apostolic, the more he is also free and the more he understands from within and willingly encourages the free initiatives of his brothers in making them serve the good of all.

Ministry is holy in its source because it enables the person of the bishop or priest to act in the person of Christ the Head. It is also holy in its effects: the sacramental acts of the minister produce their effects not by reason of the disposition of the minister nor of the recipients, but by reason of the act of Christ that the sacrament signifies and effects or, as we say, *ex opere operato,* by reason of the work accomplished by Christ himself. This is due to the nature of the priesthood of Christ and, consequently, to that of the sacraments of the New Covenant.

Because Christ does not offer a sacrifice apart from himself but offers himself, his sacrifice is eternal and his act of offering is done once and for all. It is therefore efficacious, and this efficacy does not depend on the disposition of the faithful, as it did in the "sacraments" of the Old Covenant. By his baptism the believer is made a participant in the priesthood of Christ, and the priestly ministry makes it known that the efficacy of the sacraments comes only from Christ the High Priest. It is one and the same thing to be configured to Christ the Head and to let the act of Christ produce its effect. *In persona Christi Capitis* and *ex opere operato* are inseparably joined. The first makes the minister an apostle in the full sense; the second places the minister in the service of the Spirit's power. By virtue of the first principle, the Church of Christ, not a *congregatio,* exists; by virtue of the second principle, the grace of Christ acts through his minister, without the minister influencing the efficacy of grace in any way. The efficacy of grace does not depend on the minister's worthiness: Saint Augustine definitively established this principle in opposition to the Donatist point of view.

The priesthood of the bishop and priest is therefore a ministry, but this ministry is not a function; it is a mission. The grace by which bishop and priest are placed in the service of the Church invests their person and requires it for the ministry so that it becomes a source of sanctification: ministry sanctifies. The more the priest and the bishop are sanctified, the more their brothers see in them Christ, leader and head of his Church, interceding for them and for all men, and so they experience the efficacy of grace and are transformed. There is a priestly charism.

At the end of the French Revolution, which had, at the social level, shown the effects of enlightened reason, this charism shone in the Curé of Ars. By prayer, preaching and catechism, by the celebration of Mass and of the sacraments, and by care for all his parishioners and the poor he transformed his parish. Moreover, the charism of reconciliation and absolution, which he received and exercised to an eminent degree, transformed the hearts of thousands every year for thirty years. Ars became a place of pilgrimage during the lifetime of Jean-Marie Vianney and remains so today. To the grace of the priesthood, a modern man reacts like medieval man and man of ancient times. He agrees with Origen and Augustine about requiring priests and bishops to be holy and about chastising those who flee this demand: those who prefer their own benefits to the good of their flocks, are mercenaries, not shepherds. So the idea of ministry does not abolish the ideal of pastoral holiness; it emphasizes it.

We may ask ourselves if, since the most recent council, this ideal, which sparked the renewal of the Council of Trent, has not been downplayed. Is the object of pastoral action to incarnate the holiness of the pastor or to offer him projects for pastoral action? This question determines the type of formation before and after ordination, the personal style of life and the style of cooperation among priests themselves and with the laity. Like every Christian, the priest is free with the freedom that the Holy Spirit gives in making him a son of God freed from the slavery of sin, and this freedom is placed in the service of his brothers. The priest is able to say to his brothers: "Free like you, I am your servant." This does not diminish freedom, as I will explain, but orients it and sets its boundaries. We can see these boundaries set in two directions:

beginning with God and toward the faithful. Beginning with God: the candidate is called by the Lord through his bishop to ministry. He follows the Lord because the Lord sends him among men as their servant. The *sequela Christi* is a requirement of ministry. Thus the bishop has authority over his priests by reason of their common ministry. Likewise, celibacy is required (according to the Tradition of the Latin Church) by reason of ministry. Nothing prevents the Church from ordaining married men and requiring continence of them from the time of ordination, as the Church did until the seventh century. Neither the obedience nor the chastity of the priest is identical to that of the religious, who is called by the Lord to follow him. I am not asking for a change in the discipline. I am showing what the freedom of the priest is, beginning with God.

What is his freedom in his relationship to the faithful? Throughout his entire life the priest manifests in his person the *unity* that is in the Lord seated at the right hand of God and, as well, the efficacy of the act of Christ. What's more, he cannot assume commitments that would divide the community or that would substitute human efficiency for spiritual efficacy. Ministry therefore determines a state of life that incarnates priestly freedom. To become in his way of living and acting the priest he has become by the grace of God is the secret of a priest's freedom and of his happiness. I would now like to recall the power of such freedom in the exercise of priestly ministry.

3. PRIESTLY TASKS

Priests and bishops announce the Word of God that the Church teaches, celebrate and administer the sacraments, and govern the people of God. They do not perform these three principal tasks exteriorly but commit themselves in them. In teaching, they do not express opinions but make heard the living Word of God, no less present in their words than in Palestine and no less active now than then; and they make it heard by ears that are capable of hearing because the Spirit speaks to them interiorly. They then also listen to their hearers, not to seek their approval or to please them, but to know concretely this living Word of God and to learn the words expressing it. This is especially true for homilies.

A homily is not a mini-course on exegesis; it does not use the Sacred Scripture as an occasion for public speeches, even if apt. Nor is it a monologue in which the orator announces his opinions. It is a liturgical act: it is the Lord Jesus who today speaks to his disciples through the mouth of the priest. It is his mystery that must be proposed for the prayer of the faithful, first of all by making known the story: the word of life is especially contained in the Gospel, in the words and gestures of the Lord. Next, the mystery is set forth by showing the intimate connection between the first and third readings, taken most often from the Old and New Testaments—this relation only rarely becomes evident to the listeners during the eucharistic celebration. By shedding light on it the priest helps his brothers enter into the mystery of Jesus, his life in God present in the Church. The impressive unity between the Old and New Testaments gives evidence for the fundamental declarations of biblical revelation.[4]

This being explained, the concrete applications, so varied according to the place, age and character of the listeners, will not apply the counsels of a common morality, that of the group or of the society, but will invite people to live more fully the life of Christ by humbly welcoming it. This system, flexible yet firm, allows each person to find and express what is essential according to his taste and grace, because it is liturgical and allows the priest to stay within the liturgical action instead of breaking out to make a speech. If it is a liturgical, priestly act, the homily expresses a working word: through it, the Lord Jesus acts in souls and unites the assembly.

There is nothing more simple and less monotonous than a

[4] Hans Urs von Balthasar, *Das Licht des Wortes* (Light of the Word: A Commentary on the Sunday Readings) (Trier: Paulinus Verlag, 1987).

liturgical celebration. Let us take the Eucharist. It begins with "In the name of the Father, and of the Son, and of the Holy Spirit", and with the greeting of Christ: "Peace be with you" or "The Lord be with you". It is the memorial of the Lord done in his name. The priest celebrates it *in persona Christi Capitis* and lets the Spirit work through his ministry. Everything is received, coming from the depths of time, and transmitted until the Lord comes again. It is, then, a Eucharist, that of the Lord, who places it in our hands. Everything is living and a source of life, of the eternal life that is given us from this moment on and already transfigures our mortal existence. Everything is marked with dignity. The priest is beforehand submissive to such a dignity because of the grace of the priesthood. It is up to him to be adapted to it interiorly as well as exteriorly by his vestments, gestures and words. What is pedestrian takes away from the dignity of the liturgy and, consequently, from the dignity of the ministerial priesthood. The two, in effect, hold fast together. Where the consciousness of the dignity of the priesthood wanes, the liturgical celebration also loses its dignity. By *dignity* I mean neither something overly hieratic, the enemy of simplicity, nor a respectability translated into a gravity of performance. The dignity of which I speak here reflects in the celebration the glory of God who communicates himself to his children. It also proceeds from the adoration of this glory. It is like a sphere in which the life of Christ is received and offered in thanksgiving. It is the opposite of pharisaism. Where it diminishes, pharisaism grows: the life of Christ is no longer guided by the law of the Spirit but according to human law, that of the Old Testament or that of conscience—in one form or another, man resolves to control what comes from God. If we put liturgical law in opposition to the spontaneity of the assembly and of the priest, we would no longer understand that the priest acts *in persona Christi Capitis* and that the Lord himself acts through his sacramental rites. The assembly would become conscious of itself rather than of the presence of the Lord, and the efficacy of the sacraments would depend on the disposition of the members of the assembly. Nothing would remain but *ex opera operantis* —the *ex opere operato* has disappeared. We would then begin to measure the quality of the celebrations. The *congregatio* would no longer be a *convocatio.* It is a responsibility of the priest and of the bishop to see that the meeting of the brothers be an assembly convoked by the Lord, that is, be the Church.

The ministry of reconciliation is essential to the community and to priests. God alone forgives and, in forgiving, establishes the New Covenant in Christ. The Church is established to announce and to grant the forgiveness that renews the heart and the world. The priest exercises the ministry of reconciliation through teaching, through the sacraments (especially that of penance) and through governing. In all things he teaches that God the Trinity, who created us in his Son to make us all sons, has saved us from sin and from eternal death through his life, because of which he could not spare his only Son. The ethic that flows from this is then an ethic of pardon or of grace. Today there exist moral doctrines that define natural law, conscience, sin and judgment but that put aside or leave in the shadows the forgiveness and grace of God. One can understand how, in reaction to doctrines that are too subjective or based on calculation, one must strain to understand better what is intrinsically evil. Yet one would hardly stay on track if what is intrinsically evil were not perceived as sin in the light of forgiveness. We only know evil as sin in the act that frees us from it. Beyond that there are nothing but preliminary, necessary considerations, as necessary as the Old Testament. All that precedes the light of God's forgiveness in the New is found in the shadow of the Old. If one presented the Old as such, the ethic would be pharisaical. It would close hearts to the Spirit, who is the forgiveness of sins, and dislocate the ministry of reconciliation. By this means and by still others, the menace of pharisaism threatens to corrode the Church. Laxism and rigorism, which tore consciences apart in the seventeenth and eighteenth centuries, could well tear them apart in the twenty-first century. They are two contrary elements of the same pharisaism because they place the "I" either above or below the law instead of welcoming the law of the Spirit with a humble heart. The Spirit of Christ requires the whole man, since God gave everything in his Son; to put oneself above or below the law is simply to side step this requirement. The priest is called to exhort his brothers without tiring: "That they may have a simple heart before God, without demands and thus without resentment (since Baius and Nietzsche man has learned to demand things from God); and that they may forgive one another as God has forgiven their trespasses" (that is the fifth petition of the *Pater Noster* that Jesus explained so often).

When he listens to his brothers and sisters in confession, it is toward this simplicity of heart that he will lead them and to which he will exhort them. Through the priest's ministry, God himself listens to them. He recognizes through the priest the sins that have wounded his Son and put him to death. Thus the priest will help his brothers and sisters to confess sins, not states of soul or more or less evil dispositions. He will ask in one way or another; What is bad and has offended God in what you have done? He will thereby help them form their consciences. Some, helped in such a way, will then declare, "I am proud" or "I am lustful." The priest will teach them that in confession one uses the past tense: "I was proud in doing this or that." If not, the heart is not open to God; it sees itself and hates itself out of spite. He thus teaches his brothers to view their pasts the way God views what his Son did for mankind. He will do all this with discretion and sobriety, measuring himself by what each soul is capable of understanding and bearing; this will lead him at times to be silent. Between the accusation and the sin as God forgives it there is one thing more that is not measured: the priest is the witness to it.

As minister, this one thing more is put on his shoulders; according to the measure of his grace, he has the freedom to draw from it to lead his brother to simplicity of heart and also to take upon himself something of the burden that Christ carries. This freedom is given to him in the communion of saints. To give to the penitent a share in the knowledge that God has of sin is thus the goal of the exhortation, preceded by a requisite questioning.

I have been astonished to notice that I have attained this goal by repeating word for word all or part of the confession. What was still subjective in the confession had become objective. The penitent then begins to perceive the gravity of his act. Perhaps he would like to diminish it. If the confession was well made, we will not help him in this. The penitent thus enters into the forgiveness of God, who reveals to him the gravity of his sin. The forgiveness of God is, in effect, what is essential. The exhortation prepares the reception of forgiveness for what it is: God forgives; that means God transforms sin into a source of grace, to the extent that where sin left its after-effects, there precisely is where grace will be at work with the penitent. Henceforth the penitent is able to and does have confidence in this grace, instead of fearing to fall again because of his weakness. This confidence in God belongs to the penitential attitude, according to the expression of Adrienne von Speyr in her beautiful book on confession.[5] The penance or satisfaction that the priest imposes obviously is not proportionate to the sin committed. It joins the penitent with the sacrificial act of Christ and with the prayers of the Virgin Mary and the saints for this penitent. It will also be adapted as much as possible to the spiritual necessities of the penitent. It will help him keep himself in the penitential attitude.

I have perhaps spoken too much of the ministry of reconciliation. I will be brief on the subject of governing. I have, in effect, already stated what, in my view, is essential.

Although by human necessity bishops and priests must perform administrative tasks, they are not administrators. Their first task is to contribute to the growth, not of diocesan and parochial works, but of that divine life in the brothers who are entrusted to them, and with their brothers they take care to incarnate this growing life. Authority, according to the etymology of *auctoritas*, is in the service of growth. Thus, pastors are fathers; Paul and the Tradition proclaim it. It is by being in the service of their brothers, by winning their confidence, that they exercise their spiritual fatherhood. Origen, Ambrose, Augustine and Jean-Marie Vianney are the shining links of an immense chain. Offices and commis-

---

[5] Adrienne von Speyr, *Confession* (San Francisco: Ignatius Press, 1985).

sions for vocations are worth nothing without fatherhood. The priest engenders the priest, and not only the priest but the male and female religious and other charisms in the Church. This is why the governing is paternal. "Love your priests", Jean-Marie Vianney advises his new bishop who came to him to confess. He did not give him any other advice. "Love your brothers" and your governing will be paternal without being paternalistic; this would be the only advice one could give to a priest who asks God to purify him. Too many communities lack this paternal governing.

4. THE SPHERES IN WHICH MINISTRY IS EXERCISED

Several actions of the triple ministry of teaching, of sanctifying and of governing having been characterized, what is left to consider are the spheres in which the priest exercises his ministry and the ways he is able to exercise it within those spheres. I will distinguish three spheres: that of the relationship between the person and nature, that of the relationship between human persons and that of the relationship between man and God.

Since the eighteenth century, the relationship between the person and nature has been characterized as a project of dominating nature, which has been considered an object of science and technique. This project influences the manner of organizing and distributing goods, that is to say, economics; and economics in turn influences the manner of organizing the relationship between work and consumption. This chain of relationships, created by enlightened reason, produced the great ecological and social questions. From that time the human consciousness of a *respect* for nature and for man as worker and consumer has grown. *To respect* means to treat nature and man *by reason* of what nature *is* and by reason of what the person is who works and consumes to provide for the necessities of life, not *in function* of the *utility* that one can obtain from nature and from the person who works and consumes.

Respect for the worker is determined by social justice, respect for nature by temperance, respect for the consumer by both.

Social doctrine will, in the future, extend to the rights and duties of the consumer. Cosmology, strongly neglected in education, will learn to understand the world created by the Word and recapitulated in Christ; and the ecological ethic will inculcate respect for nature. The coming generations will be less tempted to concentrate on man while forgetting the created world. Liturgical celebration, which succumbed to this temptation especially since the Council, will rediscover the splendor that comes to it from the celestial Church and its natural symbols, for it is in the liturgy that the created world is celebrated instead of being exploited. Poverty will also have the fullness that Saint Francis of Assisi gave it: there will not only be, as we have seen these past decades, solidarity with the poor, but also a simplicity of heart that receives all creation from God—man and all of nature already reconciled by the Crucified One. Such poverty leaves its mark on justice and temperance; it opens justice to mercy and places the fire of the Cross in temperance.

The relationship between man and his fellow man belongs par excellence to the political sphere, which has as its object not the administration of things but the government of people. The relationship between man and woman is at the center of human, and therefore political, relations. This relationship between man and woman is natural because of sexual reproduction and is open to God through conjugal love. Like all natural things, it is the object of science and technique. The mastery these can give to man and woman in sexual reproduction allows them better to attain the end of reproduction, but also permits them to enslave these scientific and technical means to their particular desires without respect for nature—that is, without ordering them to their proper end inscribed in their created nature. Man and woman thus have the means to close their love in on themselves. Such a love, without God, loses the sense of sexual difference, for this is the immediately sensible sign of the finitude of the human being and of his incapacity to fulfill himself by himself. Sexual difference having been lost, homosexuality ceases to be a fact and becomes a right. Femininity developing in such a context encounters two temptations: to affirm the right of the woman over her womb, and to hold to an equality of woman and man that ignores the sense of sexual difference.

In such a world, the priest will be of service only if he holds fast in his heart to a few convictions. First, conjugal moral problems do not end in the private sphere but determine political society: laws on abortion and future laws on bioethical questions attest to this. The good of conjugal union is no less important than social justice—being essential to society, it is eminently social. Second, the teaching of the Church concerning conjugal morality brings incomparable enlightenment to human persons. It prevents them from despairing over love, the fault of trying to find sense in a love that is deprived, on account of the absence of God, and filled with the demiurge project of dominating nature. Third, the divine constitution of the Church gives the relationship between man and woman its definitive foundation: Christ the Head, in effect, unites himself to the Church his Bride. This union allows a better understanding of the common or personal priesthood and the ministerial priesthood, the marian Church and the hierarchical Church as well as the organic and personal link between the Mother of God and the priest. It is important in our cultural context to grow in such an understanding. Finally, priestly celibacy in such a world attests that the fertility of a man is consecrated to his ministry and that his capacity to love contributes to represent the love of Christ for his Church. It is a sign of contradiction as much as it is a calling.

Let us continue with the third sphere, that of the relationship between man and God. Today, one who believes is suspected of integralism, of fundamentalism, of fanaticism. The dominant culture has lost its sense of the religious. For this reason, it has lost its own roots, it is in the process of losing itself; barbarism gains ground in the most rational societies. The revelation of God attested to in the Scriptures of the Old and New Testaments reawakens the sense of the religious by making God known. Through the Holy Spirit it inspires understanding itself. Henri de

Lubac taught us in *Medieval Exegesis*[6] to remember that this understanding of the Sacred Scripture was prevalent until the sixteenth century. While appearing according to different modalities, this understanding remains what it was. One sees this in a Schlier or in a Riesenfeld. Thus, it is to this understanding of the Scriptures that future priests should be initiated. Thanks to it, they will be able to give a homily, teach the Word of God, and celebrate liturgy. They will be able to make heard the questions of God for man, which go farther than the questions of man for God. By beginning on this track a culture could once again be born or develop.

Such an understanding requires docility toward the Holy Spirit, who operates in the priest in his obedience to his bishop and the pope. There is a mystery in the priesthood: the life of a man is directly overtaken by the burden that is placed on his shoulders. This mystery is that of Jesus, who expressed in human terms the will of the Father even in that which is opposed to him: it is obedience that joined the Son to the Father. It is also obedience that allows the priest humanly to bear the weight that is imposed on him.

Therefore, to each sphere of ministry corresponds an attitude and an understanding: to the economic sphere, poverty and the understanding of cosmology, of social doctrine, and of an ecological ethic; to the political sphere, chastity and a positive adherence to the conjugal morality taught by the Church; to the supernatural sphere, obedience and understanding of Sacred Scripture.

---

[6] *Exégèse médiévale: Les quatre sens de l'Ecriture,* 3 vols. (Paris: Aubier-Montaigne, 1959).

A RESPONSE TO
REV. GEORGES CHANTRAINE, S.J.

By Msgr. Richard K. Malone, S.T.D., J.C.L.

The discussion of the priesthood in recent years (seventies and eighties) has revolved around two areas: whether the source should be christological or pneumatological, whether the activity and the person should be described in functional or in ontological terms.

Fr. Chantraine maintains a rich trinitarian viewpoint throughout his paper. Indeed, we want to maintain a trinitarian viewpoint that will take into account a christological foundation and will do justice to the christological concreteness of salvation history. At the same time we need an adequate theological definition that provides for the richness of the personal action of the Spirit. In a fully trinitarian concept of the priesthood these two would not become exclusive options but would be joined together in a more inclusive fashion. Fr. Chantraine's viewpoint allows this to take place.

The christological foundation of the Church's ministry means that salvation has been given to the Church through Jesus Christ, that the Word of God is not received from below but rather is graciously bestowed and requires a commission in order to be announced officially.

Here, by the way, we should notice Fr. Chantraine's further consideration on the differences between the *convocatio* and the *congregatio*. The *convocatio* is again trinitarian in its source and effects.

The Church and the ministry have a given norm to which they must constantly redirect themselves, namely, Jesus Christ.

The christological foundation for the ministry is thus not only an ideological legitimation of ministry under certain circumstances, but also a criterion for, and on certain occasions, a critique of the concrete praxis of the ministry.

Some theologians think that, as essential and constitutive as ministry is for the community, there is no essential difference between laypersons and ministers. They think that a ministry is not a state of life but rather a function. Only in the Middle Ages does it begin to appear as a state of life rather than as an official service in the community; it was personalized and, in a sense, privatized.

By reason of this functional attitude these theologians reject the ontological quality of the person of the minister independently of the constitutive ecclesial context. For example, for Fr. Edward Schillebeeckx, O.P., the understanding of the ministry as a function does not mean that the minister is a mere functionary or a mere mouthpiece of the community. He must take the lead in the community by really following Christ, i.e., by Christian praxis. Solidarity in suffering with the poor and lowly is, above all, an essential mark of the apostolicity of the ministry.

No one will dispute that the representatives of Christ, through their living and following of Christ, make the work of ministry convincing and persuasive. The scandalous division between official mission or function and personal life has always been taken as an extreme case in traditional theology. In his paper Fr. Chantraine uses the category of consecration and mission as a way to bridge any hint of division between the function and the life of the minister.

Fr. Chantraine has mentioned the debate between Augustine and the Donatists over the proper understanding of the holiness of the Church and its ministers. At that time the Church decided in favor of Augustine, that the holiness of the ministry is not founded on the personal holiness of the minister but on the gift of grace and the commission that is given him by Jesus Christ in the Holy Spirit, which precedes his own activity. This is the ontological understanding of Church and ministry as set against a purely charismatic understanding.

The inner basis of the "ontological" understanding consists in the fact that Jesus Christ, as Head of the Body and High Priest of the Church, is himself the primary proclaimer, distributor of the sacraments, celebrant of the liturgy, shepherd and gatherer of the community—as Fr. Chantraine noted in referring to the *convocatio*—who works through the priest, and in certain borderline cases, for the safety of the community and individuals, even through a bad priest.

For many of us who feel unequal to the high claims that our ministry imposes on us, precisely this "ontological" understanding is a help and a consolation because we can say to ourselves that the salvation of our parishes and of the many persons entrusted to us does not ultimately depend on our accomplishments or success. This is also a consolation for many communities. Nor does this allow us to take refuge in quietism; it spurs us to generous cooperation with Christ's activity in us.

We can say, paradoxically, that for that very reason a priest's activity is pure service to another; it is always more than his own service, i.e., more than his human and Christian praxis. But it must try to be that too.

It is precisely when the priest understands function not as just an external functional quality but as something that draws a person so completely into service that it stamps him in his very nature and ontologically determines his person, not as something added on to the persons's essential functions and relationships, but rather *in them.*

The ontological meaning of the sacramental character signifies that the priest's commission from Jesus Christ and the promise that is entrusted to him along with it stamp the priest in his very nature and take him up into the service of Christ in his whole person.

Fr. Chantraine draws on Fr. Hans Urs von Balthasar's theology of the form. As a brief overview, we need to think for a moment of the Catholic theology of icons. We affirm that the uncircumscribed became circumscribed and that the unlimited limited himself for us. This means that the Son of God presented a form that could see and grasp. He could find hints of this in the New Testament; for example, in Philippians 2:6 we find Christ described as being in the *form* of God (*en morphe Theou*), emptying himself and taking the *form* of a servant (*en morphe doulou*). A further classic case would be the vision of the Transfiguration. We see that the apostles, who already saw something of the form of God in Christ, were admitted to an even fuller vision of Christ in the form of God. This vision gave them the light that further refined and broadened their vision so that they could, or should, see the form of God in Christ in the events of the paschal mystery. Fr. Chantraine relies on this theology of the form or living image of Christ.

Fr. Chantraine speaks to us of the priest's bearing *the form and the image* of Christ the Shepherd of the Church and image of the Father in the context of a question about the priest's unworthiness. He responds to the question, Who can represent the Lord as shepherd and head of the community? It is not his mother nor any who shine through the gift of grace, but those whom he chose and sent, among them Judas and Peter. He tells us that the apostolic Church shows us the disfigured face of the Lord, yet this humiliated Jesus is the life-giving Lord. He also states that such a configuration to Christ glorified, who remains in the Church as the Suffering Servant, is a grace conferred by the Lord himself at the Last Supper. He speaks again of our need to see in the Church's countercultural claims on the level of priesthood the mystery of the Cross itself: we should look on him whom they have pierced.

In another place, when he distinguishes between the *congregatio* and the *convocatio,* he states that only those who have the grace of the priesthood have the capability of manifesting Christ the Head of his Church and image of the Father in the midst of his own. So they alone can manifest this eternal choice and make visible the trinitarian love in history. They are sent among the community to summon the people to God and to send the baptized sons and daughters on their own missions.

The priest is to be understood as a living image of Christ the Shepherd, one who receives the form of Christ the Servant and glorious High Priest and who is to be no countersign or contradictory form—a satanic image. Ontology leads to ethical praxis. The priest's call is to follow Christ; the *sequela Christi* is the norm of his ethical behavior as living image of Christ the Shepherd. We find this call in the final image of Peter in John's Gospel, 21:18ff:

> Truly, truly, I say to you, when you were young, you guided yourself and walked where you would; but when you are old, you will stretch out your hands, and another will find you and carry you where you do not wish to go . . . and, after this, he said to him, "Follow me".

This following of Christ and the law of the Spirit are to come to visibility in the priest's service of sacramentally imaging Christ the High Priest and Shepherd. We can also speak of the priestly charism as *leading to* a subjective identity in Christ and point to the remarkable way it became visible in the personality of the Curé of Ars.

As living image of Christ the Head of his Body and Shepherd of his flock, the priest is empowered to act sacramentally and called ethically to follow the Christ in whose name he acts ecclesiastically.

I want to suggest a reflection that will offer a way out of the dilemma: Is our morality a morality of the natural law or of the Spirit and grace? How do these work together without losing their specific characters?

It seems that the starting point should be the Christian believer himself who uses practical reason, the Sermon on the Mount and the inner law of the Spirit (Rm 8) for his moral life. Both reason and grace are given by God the Creator and Redeemer for our good and our salvation. When we think of practical reason, we need to think of a dynamic reason at work in the hands of a believer who also experiences a natural desire for the vision of God and all the dynamism this entails. All of this—reason, natural desire, transformation by grace—is given by the one God. Reason and grace work in us to activate the natural desire and allow it to shape our desires and direct them toward the full realization of the Good, which is God. "Our hearts are restless until they rest in you."

I think this is born out of one Lord's practice in the synoptic

Gospels, e.g., in the meeting with the rich young man. The Lord proposes the Ten Commandments to him. Then he offers the young man the path of poverty and of following him more closely: "If you wish to be perfect, sell all you have and come follow me". Not that the law of the commandments could be observed without empowerment by the Spirit, but that the Lord now gives the Spirit for this and for its inner intentionality, plus a recognition that Christ is the total good, the end and purpose of the law.

A practical question in the training of seminarians would be, What are the special qualities that we would look for and wish to cultivate in this theology of the priest as image of Christ the Head of the Body and image of the Father's gathering together of the children of God? Should we think that priests are ordained social workers who are adept at gathering the community together in the way mayors or politicians do? Or do we look for qualities of a spiritual and theological nature that will allow priests to give spiritual and moral leadership to their communities?

DR. WILLIAM E. MAY

PEOPLE'S NEEDS, MORAL TRUTHS AND PRIESTS

INTRODUCTION

My intention here is to consider the indispensable role that priests have to play in serving the real needs of their people: helping people in their endeavor to discover moral truth. I will begin with a discussion of people's needs, then take up the question of moral truths and their relationship to people's needs. I will conclude by commenting on the role of the priest as moral guide.

I. PEOPLE'S NEEDS

In his book *Love and Responsibility*, Karol Wojtyla declared:

> We must demand from a person, as a thinking individual, that his or her ends should be genuinely good, since the pursuit of evil ends is contrary to the rational nature of the person.... Indeed, the purpose of education ... is just that: a matter of seeking true ends, i.e., real goods as the ends of our actions.[1]

What has talk about "ends" and "real goods" to do with people's needs? The relationship between the two is obvious.

[1] Karol Wojtyla, *Love and Responsibility,* trans. H. J. Willetts (New York: Farrar, Straus, Giroux, 1981), 27.

What people most need are the goods perfective of them. *Good* has the connotation of fullness of being. Thus a "good" car is one that operates well and does what cars are supposed to do: efficiently and safely move people from here to there. Human beings, when they come into existence, are not yet "finished products", as it were. They are not yet the beings they are meant to be. They are not yet their full "selves". But how do they become such? They become such by participating ever more fully in the goods perfective of them. Indeed, deep within the being of human persons are "natural" inclinations or tendencies, dynamic sources of endeavor, I would call them, that orient them to the goods perfective of them.

This is something that the Catholic tradition has long recognized. Saint Thomas Aquinas, for example, wrote that there is a triple-tiered set of "natural inclinations" dynamically pointing human persons toward the goods perfective of them. The first set includes the inclination that human beings, insofar as they are substantial entities, have toward the preservation of their own being; and because life is the being of living things, the good to which this dynamic tendency inclines us is the good of human life itself. The second set includes the inclination that orients human persons, as animals whose survival as a species depends on sexual reproduction, to hand on the good of life to new human persons and to provide these new human persons with homes where they can take root and grow; the relevant good here is the good of human life in its transmission and education. The third set includes the natural tendency of human persons to pursue truth, to live together with others in fellowship and justice and to be reasonable in making choices; the relevant goods here are the goods of knowledge of the truth, friendship and justice and the good that can be called "practical reasonableness".[2]

Saint Thomas' list of natural inclinations and of the goods corresponding to them is not intended by him to be taxative but illustrative, as indicated by his use of such expressions as "and the

---

[2] ST, I–2, 94, 2.

like" (*et similia*) in referring to them. His basic point is that these goods, when grasped by practical reason, serve as "starting points" or principles for deliberating about what we are going to do. The goods to which we are naturally inclined and that human reason "naturally"—i.e., spontaneously—grasps as the "ends" of human action are all real goods of human persons. They are the goods that we prize and do not price. They are goods *of* persons, intrinsically perfecting them; they are not goods *for* persons, merely useful or instrumental goods, like my suit or this building. Human persons *need* these goods to be fully the beings God wills them to be.

Germain Grisez has sought to build on the foundations that Saint Thomas laid, and a brief summary of his account of human goods will be helpful. Grisez attempts to provide an exhaustive, not merely illustrative, list of the goods perfective of human persons. In developing his account Grisez first distinguishes between two broad types of goods perfective of human persons. Goods of the first sort, which he calls "existential" or "reflexive", depend for their intelligibility and existence on human choices; choice, in other words, enters into their very definition. Such goods are perfective of human persons insofar as the persons are gifted with free choice. Goods of the second sort, which he calls "substantive", perfect other dimensions of human persons; choice does not enter into their definition or intelligibility. But the goods in question, whether "existential" or "substantive", are real goods perfective of human persons, making them "to be" more fully.[3]

Grisez says that the theme common to existential goods is that of harmony. First, there is the harmony within the self called self-integration, the good in which we participate when we "put ourselves together" and overcome internal tension and disunity. Second, there is the harmony consisting in the agreement between practical insight, will and conduct; this is the good of practical

---

[3] Germain Grisez, *The Way of the Lord Jesus,* vol. 1 of *Christian Moral Principles* (Chicago: Franciscan Herald Press, 1983), 123–24.

reasonableness or authenticity. Third, there is the harmony meant to exist between us and other persons, the goods of justice and friendship and peace. Finally, fourth, there is the harmony meant to exist between ourselves and God, the good of religion or of friendship with God. These goods are existential "because they fulfill persons insofar as persons make free choices and are capable of moral good and evil".[4] These goods, in other words, depend for both their intelligibility and existence on human choice. We cannot pull ourselves together unless we choose to do so; we cannot act in conformity with our own best judgments unless we choose to do so; we cannot be friends with others, respect them as persons, unless we so choose; we cannot be God's friends unless we choose to do so.

The substantive goods of human persons are, fifth, those of bodily life and health, including bodily integrity, goods that fulfill us as human beings; sixth, knowledge of the truth and appreciation of beauty, goods that fulfill us as intelligent beings; and, seventh, playful activities and skillful performances, goods that fulfill us as makers and sharers in culture. While these goods can be *caused* by human choices (we can choose to live healthily, choose to pursue knowledge and so forth), they do not depend on human choice in order to be understood— choice does not enter into their very definition. Yet these are really goods of human persons, perfective of them. Moreover, there is a deep relationship between the "existential" and the "substantive" goods. The substantive goods are the "stuff" of or vehicles for the existential goods. If we choose to be friends with others, we surely will that they be alive, that they be healthy, that they develop their intelligence and come to know the truth and so on. In and through our choices and actions, we can help others participate in these goods; we can help them to be healthy, we can protect their lives, we can instruct them and enable them to participate ever more fully in the goods of knowledge of the truth and the appreciation of beauty

[4] Ibid., 124.

and the other goods. We are, in addition, friends of God, not by saying "I love you", but by bringing forth works of love, works that enable others to share in the substantive goods of human existence.[5]

Persons are said to be good in an unqualified sense if and only if they are morally good. Moral good consists essentially in one's choices; a person is considered morally good not because he makes a few good choices but only because he makes a set of such choices and lives by them consistently. Moral goodness is within one's power, with the help of God's grace; and moral goodness is an essential part of integral human fulfillment, of being fully the beings God wills us to be. This is clearly the teaching of the Church, as a brief examination of some key texts from Vatican II will make evident.

The Council distinguished two kinds of dignity proper to human beings. The first is the dignity we have by virtue of being human beings to begin with, creatures made in the image and likeness of God. This dignity is God's gift, and by reason of it a human person is a being of moral worth, with a dignity that surpasses in value the entire material order. But there is a second kind of dignity proper to human persons. This is the dignity to which we are called as intelligent and free beings, capable of determining our lives by our own free choices. This is the dignity that we are to give to ourselves, with the help of God's unfailing grace, by freely choosing to shape our lives and actions in accord with the truth. It is the dignity we give to ourselves when, through our choices, we participate in the "existential" goods of human existence.

According to Vatican II "the highest norm of human life is the divine law—eternal, objective, and universal—whereby God orders, directs, and governs the entire universe and all the ways of the human community by a plan conceived in wisdom and love." In addition, the Council Fathers continued, "man has been made by God to participate in this law, with the result that, under the

[5] Ibid.

gentle disposition of divine providence, he can come to perceive
ever increasingly the unchanging truth".[6]

This passage, taken from *Dignitatis Humanae,* concludes by saying
that "on his part man perceives and acknowledges the imperatives
of the divine law through the mediation of conscience".[7] The
role of conscience in helping us come to know the "unchanging
truth" of God's divine and eternal law and its "imperatives" is
developed in another document of the Council, *Gaudium et Spes.*
There we read:

> Deep within his conscience man discovers a law which he
> has not laid on himself but which he must obey. The voice of
> this law,[8] ever calling him to love and do what is good and
> avoid evil, tells him inwardly at the right moment, do this,
> shun that. For man has in his heart a law written by God. *His
> dignity lies in observing this law* [emphasis added], and by it he
> will be judged.[9]

Fidelity to conscience means "a search for the truth" and "true
solutions" to moral problems. Conscience, this passage notes, can
"err through invincible ignorance without losing its dignity", so
long as there is sufficient "care for the search for the true and the
good"; but "to the extent that a *correct* conscience holds sway
[emphasis added], persons and groups turn away from blind choice
and seek to conform to the *objective norm of morality* [emphasis
added]".[10]

Thus far we have seen that what people most fundamentally
need are the *goods* perfective of them. Most important, if they are
to be fully the beings God wills them to be, they need to discover
moral truth so that they will be able to shape their lives in accord

---

[6] *Dignitatis Humanae,* n. 3.

[7] Ibid.

[8] In the Abbott translation of *The Documents of Vatican II* (New York: America
Press, 1965), this passage from *Gaudium et Spes* (GS), n. 16, is incorrectly translated
as "the voice of conscience". The Latin text is *cuius vox,* with the antecedent of *cuius*
being *lex* (law), not *conscientia* (conscience).

[9] GS, n. 16.

[10] Ibid.

with it, distinguishing morally good alternatives of choice from morally bad ones, and in this way attain for themselves the dignity to which they are called as intelligent and free persons. I turn now to a consideration of human choices and moral truth.

2. HUMAN ACTIONS, HUMAN CHOICES AND MORAL TRUTH

Because of the dignity that we have as beings made in the image and likeness of God, we are endowed with freedom of choice or the capacity for self-determination. Human acts are not physical events that come and go. Rather, as Saint Thomas noted, human action is a deed that *abides* within the person.[11] For at the core of a human act is a free, self-determining choice. In and through the free choices that we make every day we give to ourselves our identity as moral beings, our character. Human actions are, as it were, "words" that human persons speak, and through them we reveal *who* we are. Through them we give to ourselves our "character", which can properly be described as "the integral existential identity of the person—the entire person in all his or her dimensions as shaped by morally good and bad choices—considered as a disposition for further choices".[12]

We are free to choose what we are to do, but we are not free to make what we choose to do to be right or wrong, good or bad. Their rightness or wrongness is determined by objective criteria or norms—truths—that we can come to know. We ought to choose in accordance with our own best judgments—that is what is meant when it is said that we ought to "follow our conscience". But our best judgments can be mistaken—and corrected. If the mistake in them is not attributable to our own negligence in seeking the truth, we do not make ourselves to be evildoers in

[11] ST, I-2, 57, 4.
[12] Grisez, *Christian Moral Principles,* 61.

choosing to act in accord with our judgments, even if what we choose to do is not, by reason of its object, what we ought to do. Moreover, our judgments will be "correct", i.e., true, if they are made in accord with objective criteria or norms.

In short, we have the gift of free choice, of self-determination. Choice is possible only when there are alternatives from which to choose, i.e., intelligible proposals that we can adopt by choice and execute through our deeds. But it is possible to choose wrongly as well as rightly, and choice proceeds from deliberation. Thus it must be possible to determine, prior to choice, which alternatives are morally good and which are morally bad. This determination is the work of our intelligence or capacity to know the truth. Moral norms, therefore, are truths meant to guide our choices so that we can be fully the beings we are meant to be. They are not arbitrarily imposed rules intended to curtail our liberty to do as we please. But what are these truths, and how do we discover them?

We have seen already that there are basic goods perfective of human persons and that our practical reason spontaneously grasps these goods as the "points" or "ends" of human action. Whatever we do, whether it is morally right or morally wrong, is chosen and done because we think that by so acting we will, eventually, participate in some real human good. Consequently, the first principles of practical reasoning, which direct us to pursue the goods perfective of us as human persons, are principles of intelligent activity — and morally bad activity is rational and intelligent. Thus, these principles of practical thinking are not moral norms; they do not, of themselves, enable us to distinguish between morally good and morally bad choices. Everyone, the morally perverse as well as the morally upright, recognizes these principles and appeals to them. What then are the principles or truths that enable us to tell which alternatives of choice are morally good and which are morally bad?

Here I suggest that we look for guidance from Saint Thomas Aquinas, Vatican II and the thought of some contemporary scholars — Germain Grisez and John Finnis — who seek to develop and clarify the thought of the Common Doctor and the Council.

Saint Thomas, in an article devoted to showing that all the moral precepts of the Old Law could be reduced to the ten precepts of the Decalogue, taught that the twofold law of love of God and love of neighbor, while not included among the precepts of the Decalogue, nonetheless intimately pertained to it insofar as the requirements of love of God and of neighbor must be regarded as "the first and common precepts of natural law". Consequently, all the precepts of the Decalogue must be referred to these two precepts, love of God and love of neighbor, as to their "common principles".[13] In other words, for Saint Thomas the first moral truth meant to guide our choices and actions is that we ought to choose in such a way that we exhibit true love of God and neighbor. This surely seems sound—and, we should remember, Thomas took for his authority the Word of our Lord as well as the voice of reason. Moreover, if we truly love God we ought to accept with joy his good gifts, the goods perfective of us as human persons. And if we love our neighbor, we surely ought to will that the goods of human existence flourish in him.

Vatican II also suggested a basic normative principle or moral truth to guide human choices and actions. After noting that human action is of critical importance precisely because it develops human persons and gives to them, by reason of its self-determining character, their identity as moral beings, the Council declared:

> Hence, the norm of human activity is this: that, in accord with the divine plan and will, it should harmonize with the genuine good of the human race, and allow men as individuals and as members of society to pursue their total vocation and fulfill it.[14]

Vatican II's formulation of the basic moral norm is another way of saying what Saint Thomas was saying when he affirmed that

[13] ST, 1–2, 100, 3, ad 1.
[14] GS, n. 35.

love of God and love of neighbor are the common and universal principles in whose light we can distinguish morally good alternatives from morally bad ones and in whose light we can then see the truth of such specific precepts as those forbidding the killing of innocents and adultery.

This fundamental moral norm is further clarified, in my judgment, by the articulation given to it by Germain Grisez, namely, that "in voluntarily acting for human goods and avoiding what is opposed to them, one ought to choose and otherwise will those and only those possibilities whose willing is compatible with a will toward integral human fulfillment".[15] By this he means that in choosing among alternatives, we ought to choose only those whose willing is compatible with a heart open to all the goods of human existence and to the persons in whom those goods are meant to flourish.

The basic moral norm, as articulated by Aquinas, Vatican II and Grisez, makes it clear that morality comes from the heart. A person who is about to choose in a morally upright way respects all the goods of human existence and listens to the appeal they make to him through all the principles of practical thinking. The morally upright person is therefore unwilling to ignore, slight, neglect, damage, destroy or impede any real good of human persons. His heart, rather, is open to all of them. He is also fair and just and realizes that the goods perfective of human persons are not his alone or his family's or his race's or his nation's. A person about to choose in a morally wrong way does not respect all the goods of human persons and the persons in whom they are meant to flourish. The alternative one is about to adopt by choice involves detriment to some human good that, we must always remember, exists in some real human person. One is tempted to will this detriment for the sake of realizing some other good that one prefers. Such an alternative is responsive to at least one principle of practical reasoning, and it might be merely irrelevant to and thus consistent with respect for others, but it is both

[15] Grisez, *Christian Moral Principles,* 184.

relevant to and inconsistent with the principle that directs one to promote and respect the good that the proposed alternative will impede or destroy or damage or set aside.[16]

Saint Thomas believed that the ten precepts of the Decalogue followed "immediately, with but little consideration", from the law of love of God and love of neighbor.[17] Moreover, he held, in company with the Catholic Tradition, that the precepts of the Decalogue, as commonly understood within the Church, are absolutely binding and exceptionless. It is *always* wrong deliberately to kill innocent human persons, to commit adultery, to steal and to perjure oneself.[18] My point here is not to consider how the precepts of the Decalogue are "derived" from the law of love of God and neighbor, but simply to note the witness of Saint Thomas to the Catholic Tradition. Today the Magisterium renders the same witness, reminding us time and time again that there are some absolute moral norms and that there are some sorts of human choices that we ought never freely make. Thus Pope John Paul II, in his apostolic exhortation *Reconciliatio et Poenitentia,* referred to a "doctrine based on the Decalogue and on the preaching of the Old Testament, and assimilated into the *kerygma* of the Apostles and belonging to the earliest teaching of the Church, and constantly reaffirmed by her up to this day". The doctrine in question is that "there exist acts which *per se* and in themselves, independently of circumstances, are always wrong by reason of their object".[19] Correspondingly, as the Holy Father noted in his "Discourse to the International Congress on Moral Theology" on April 10, 1986, "there are moral norms that have a precise content which is immutable and unconditioned[,] . . . for example

[16] On this see Germain Grisez, "Suicide and Euthanasia", *Death, Dying, and Euthanasia,* ed. Dennis Horan and David Mall (Frederick, Md.: University Publications of America, 1980), 774.

[17] ST, 1–2, 100, 1.

[18] Ibid., 100, 8. On this see Patrick Lee, "The Permanence of the Ten Commandments: St. Thomas and His Modern Commentators", *Theological Studies* (1981), 422–43.

[19] John Paul II, *Reconciliatio et Poenitentia,* n. 17.

... the norm ... which forbids the direct killing of an innocent person".[20] Indeed, it is precisely because our salvation depends on our freely choosing to shape inwardly our choices and actions in accordance with these norms that God has graciously chosen to make them known to us through his revelation—as Saint Thomas clearly teaches[21]—despite the fact that these norms can be known by the exercise of human reason. We need both to know these norms and to choose in accordance with their truth if we are to be fully the beings we are meant to be.

One might reasonably ask why the Church insists that there are absolute moral norms, normative truths that must never be cast aside. At the recent meeting of the International Theological Commission John Finnis and I together spent some time trying to articulate as clearly as possible the reasons behind this teaching. The following are the major reasons that we thought undergird this teaching (the articulation of these reasons is much more John Finnis' work than mine, and to him I am most grateful).

Each true specific moral absolute summons each person to reverence the goods intrinsic to human persons. Human persons, each in his own corporeal and spiritual unity,[22] are the only earthly creatures whom God has willed for themselves.[23] Respect for human persons, each for his own sake, is therefore required by the Creator's design and is a primary element in loving God and loving one's neighbor as oneself. Such a respect and reverence is, in addition, a primary demand of that divine dignity to which Christ has raised human nature by himself assuming it.[24]

Each true moral absolute excludes every moral choice in which, by adopting and striving after that choice's precise object, one would necessarily integrate into one's will and character some violation of, or other disrespect for, a good intrinsic to human

[20] John Paul II, "Discourse to the International Congress on Moral Theology", in *Persona, Verita e Morale* (Rome: Citta Nuova Editrice, 1987), 13, n. 4.

[21] ST, 1–2, 91, 4.

[22] GS, n. 14.

[23] Ibid., n. 24.

[24] Ibid., n. 22.

persons—oneself or another or others. Choices that adhere to the Way of Life by adhering to these moral norms and in this way reverence human persons are among the materials for the building up of the kingdom.[25] Whatever their outcome, earthly fortune or failure, these choices cultivate human personal goods (the goods of "truth and life, holiness, justice, love, and peace") and will, with these goods, be found again in the completed kingdom[26]— like Christ's adherence to his vocation in the face of earthly failure, suffering and death. The reality of this kingdom, which is being built up on earth in mystery but is not to be equated with earthly fulfillment and will not be completed save in the new heavens and the new earth,[27] is a reality that relativizes every earthly horizon one might hope to use as a "measure" for weighing the worth of possible choices. Thus the prospect of the kingdom replaces every alternative horizon against which a violation of human dignity can seem "necessary" or "the greater good" or "the lesser evil".

In fact, the norms that identify such violations of the goods intrinsic to human dignity liberate man from servitude to every partial, fragmentary and illusory horizon, from servitude to every aspiration to assume the role proper to divine Providence itself. Instead, these norms leave each person to the creativity of his own vocation, within the all-embracing vocation to holiness, the holiness that alone is adequate to the gift and promise of divine sonship and to giving and reflecting God's true glory.

In this part of my talk I have tried to identify the moral truths human persons must know if they are to meet their deepest needs and to become fully the beings they are meant to be. Now it is time to examine the indispensable role that priests play in helping people come to a knowledge of these truths.

---

[25] Ibid., n. 38.
[26] Ibid., n. 39.
[27] Ibid.

3. THE INDISPENSABLE ROLE OF PRIESTS IN MEETING PEOPLE'S NEEDS BY TEACHING MORAL TRUTHS

The priest is an officeholder in the Church. He has been "taken from among men and made their representative before God, to offer gifts and sacrifices for sins. He is able to deal patiently with erring sinners, for he himself is beset by weakness.... One does not take this honor on his own initiative, but only when called by God" (Heb 5:1-2, 4). The priest, Catholics believe, is one who acts "in the person of Christ". He acts in the person of Christ when he leads the community in the sacrifice of the Mass, the Eucharist. He acts in the person of Christ when, in the confessional, he absolves penitents from their sins and offers them moral guidance.

The priest, moreover, is "called" by a bishop and ordained by one. It is from the local ordinary that he receives the authority to celebrate the Eucharist, to hear confessions, to proclaim the Word of the Lord. Because this is so, Catholic people look to their priests for sound guidance in their moral and spiritual lives, and they are ready to accept the moral and spiritual advice of their priests as the guidance that Christ, their Lord, wishes to give them in their efforts to be fully the beings he wills them to be. Furthermore, Catholics who seek counsel from priests do so in the expectation that what they advise will be in harmony with the fundamental commitments that they, as members of the ecclesial community, have made and to which they wish to be faithful.

What ought the priest, as moral advisor, to do? I think that his principal obligation is to speak the truth. It is not to express his personal opinion or to assuage guilt or comfort a conscience. Catholics who seek the advice of a priest on a moral issue already know, I believe, that they are obliged to "follow their consciences", i.e., to act in accord with their own best judgments about what they are to do. If they were certain about what they ought to do, they would not seek the priest's advice. Thus, what they are looking for is help in *forming* their consciences, i.e., in discovering the truths that ought to guide them in making choices. It is the case, of course, that at times Catholics inclined to act in a particular way that they know is at odds with the authoritative teaching of the Church will seek out a priest precisely to support their own opinions that this teaching—e.g., on contraception—is either erroneous or at least not applicable to their own life situations. Yet they would not come to a priest for advice if they did not have some doubts about what they ought to do.

The point I am trying to make can be put this way: when a Catholic comes to a priest for moral advice he is *not* seeking an answer to a question *about* conscience, i.e., whether or not he ought to follow his own conscientious judgment of what he ought to do. He already knows that. As Germain Grisez has said, the relevant question a Catholic has in mind when he seeks the priest's counsel on moral matters is not "If I do what I think I should do but happen to be mistaken, then how do I stand [before God]?"—this is a question *about* conscience. Rather, the relevant question he has in mind is "What should I think I may do?"[28]

Consequently, a priest who begins to talk about conscience and assures the one seeking his advice that he is blameless if he sincerely thinks that what he is doing or about to do is morally all right is inappropriately replying to the real question.[29] Such priests confuse the obligation to follow one's conscience with the obligation to act in accordance with the truth. While it is true that one ought to follow one's conscience (because this is one's own best judgment about what one should do), it is not true that one's conscientious judgments make what one is about to do right or wrong. Catholics seeking moral guidance from priests are interested in the latter issue, not the former. When priests, in response to questions about the moral responsibilities of the faithful, answer that they should do what they judge right, they in effect

---

[28] Germain Grisez, "The Duty and Right to Follow One's Own Judgment of Conscience", *Homiletic and Pastoral Review* 79.7 (April 1989), 15.

[29] Ibid.

endorse subjectivism in morality and fail to respond to the questions put to them.

I fear, however, that this is at times the kind of advice that priests give to those who seek them out. What ought priests to do? As I said earlier, their principal responsibility is to speak the truth and enable their people to come to understand for themselves the true moral standards to which they ought to conform their choices and actions. Accordingly, if there are relevant teachings of the Church on the questions brought to them, priests have the obligation to present those teachings as practical truths meant to guide human choices and to show their questioners *why* these teachings are liberating truths meant to help human persons choose in such a way that they will in truth become fully the beings God wills them to be, and *not* arbitrary, legalistic impositions upon them. Thus priests have a moral obligation to teach their people that it is never right to have sex outside of marriage; that a Catholic, validly married, cannot, after divorce, truly marry another or pretend that sexual relations with another are "marital"; that it is always morally wicked to kill the innocent or to contracept, et cetera. The Church proposes these and other teachings as true, and it proposes them *in the name of Christ.* The priest is not to question these teachings. His obligation is to come to see ever more deeply the reasons these teachings are true so that he can be better prepared to help his people see for themselves that these teachings are simply requirements of love—liberating truths that enable human persons to reverence all the goods of human existence and in this way give themselves the identity of persons who truly love what is good and noble and beautiful.

If there is no clear teaching of the Church on a matter that a Catholic brings to the priest, then his obligation as a moral advisor is to help the person raise relevant moral questions about the matter at hand so that it can be determined whether adopting the proposal in question would require a choice that neglects, ignores, slights, damages, destroys or impedes in some way a good perfective of human persons.

I fear that some priests have a faulty understanding of the

words *pastoral* and *compassionate*. They rightly reject a pharasaic legalism and quite rightly refuse to lay upon their people intolerable burdens. But some priests, I think, believe that the Church's insistence on adhering to moral absolutes and on rejecting the intrinsic wickedness of certain kinds of human choices is too much for people to bear. They think, erroneously, that it is simply not possible for married couples to meet their spousal and parental responsibilities without contracepting; they think, erroneously, that it is harsh and cruel to tell a homosexually oriented person, male or female, that he or she must remain celibate, for, they contend, celibacy is a gift and this gift is not given to all. They think, erroneously, that it is insensitive, cruel and contrary to Christ's mercy to tell a divorced and remarried Catholic that he must desist from sexual relations with the "new" spouse, and so on. On these and other issues they think, erroneously, that the Magisterium's insistence on the absoluteness of some moral norms is inhuman and contrary to the gospel of the Jesus, who said, "Come to me all you who labor and are heavily burdened, for I will refresh you; for my yoke is sweet and my burden light." How, they say, can we impose on these suffering people such intolerable demands?

Such priests are gravely mistaken. Jesus' yoke is sweet and his burden is light for those who love him and the truth that he came to give us. Like his, their will is to do the will of the Father, to shape their lives in accordance with the truth, even if this means that they too must take up their cross and bear it. Catholics have, through baptism, died to sin and have risen to a new kind of life. They know that their baptismal commitment requires them to love even as they have been and are loved by God in Christ. They know that at times fidelity to Christ and his truth will cause them to suffer, but they likewise know that by uniting their lives and sufferings with Christ's they can come to share ever more deeply in his redemptive work, a work that reverences fully the great and good gifts of human existence, the goods meant to flourish in human persons, the goods protected by absolute moral norms. They know, too, that with God's unfailing grace they can choose

in ways that fully respect these goods. They want the truth, not
sentimental paternalism. And they know, deep in their hearts, that
the priest speaks the truth if and only if he affirms Church
teaching and offers them the help and support they need to make
it real in their lives.

Finally, I want to call attention to some remarks that Jacques
Maritain made concerning those in authority within a political
community, for I think that his remarks can be applied analogously
to those who hold authority in the Church—as priests do by
virtue of their authorization to act in Christ's person. Maritain
wrote:

> I just said that the representatives of the people must be
> ready to incur the displeasure of the people, if their conscience
> demands it. Now I am saying that they must carry out their
> obligations in communion with the people. Are these two
> statements contradictory? They are not, on the condition that
> this expression "in communion with the people" be correctly
> understood. In what can be called the common psyche of the
> people there is a huge variety of levels and degrees. At the most
> superficial level there are the momentary trends of opinion, as
> transient as the waves on the sea, and subjected to all winds of
> anxiety, fear, particular passions and particular interests. At the
> deeper levels, there are the real needs of the multitude. At the
> deepest level, there is the will to live together, and the obscure
> consciousness of a common destiny and vocation, and finally
> the natural trend of the human will, considered in its essence, to
> the good. Furthermore ... people are ordinarily distracted from
> their most capital aspirations and interests, as a people, by each
> one's everyday business and suffering. Under such circumstances,
> to rule in communion with the people means on the one hand
> educating and awakening the people in the very process of
> governing them, so as to demand of them, at each progressive
> step, what they themselves have been made aware of and eager
> for (I am thinking of a real work of education, grounded on
> respect for them and trust in them, and in which they are the
> principal agent ...). It means, on the other hand, being intent
> on what is deep and lasting, and most really worthy of man, in

the aspirations and psyche of the people. Thus it is that in incurring the disfavor of the people a ruler can still act in communion with the people, in the truest sense of this expression. And if he is a great ruler, he will perhaps make that endeavor into a renewed and more profound trust.[30]

These words have much to tell us, I think, about the role of the priest as a moral leader or guide. The teachings of the Magisterium are intended to remind us of who we are and what we are to do if we are to be fully the beings that we are meant to be in Christ. The priest, in his search for the truth, can best find it by accepting, with connatural eagerness, the teachings of the Church. In this way he can best meet his people's deepest needs and enable them to come to see for themselves the liberating truth of Catholic moral teaching.

RECOMMENDED READINGS

Finnis, John M. *Natural Law and Natural Rights.* Oxford and New York: Oxford University Press, 1981. chapters 3, 4 and 5 (on knowledge as a basic good, on the other basic goods and on the requirements of practical reasonableness).

——. "The Natural Law, Objective Morality, and Vatican Council II". In *Principles of Catholic Moral Life,* edited by William E. May. Chicago: Franciscan Herald Press, 1981, 113–50.

Greenburg, Thomas and John J. O'Rourke, eds. *Symposium on the Magisterium.* Boston: St. Paul Editions, 1978. Papers on the Magisterium by Archbishop John Whealon, Bishop Jeremiah Newman, William E. May and others. The papers were originally delivered at a symposium sponsored by John Cardinal Krol and the Archdiocese of Philadelphia.

[30] Jacques Maritain, *Man and the State* (Chicago: University of Chicago Press, 1951), 136–38.

Grisez, Germain. *The Way of the Lord Jesus Christ.* vol. 1 of *Christian Moral Principles.* Chicago: Franciscan Herald Press, 1983. chapter 3 (on conscience), chapter 5 (on the goods that fulfill human persons), chapter 7 (on natural law and the fundamental principle of morality), chapter 8 (on modes of responsibility), chapter 10 (on the movement from modes of responsibility to specific moral norms), chapter 35 (on the Church as moral teacher) and chapter 36 (a critique of radical theological dissent).

——. "The Duty and Right to Follow One's Own Judgment of Conscience". *Homiletic and Pastoral Review* 79.7 (April 1989), 10–16.

John Paul II. "Discourse to the International Congress on Moral Theology". In *Persona, Verità, e Morale: Atti del Congresso Internazionale di Teologia Morale (Roma 7–12 aprile 1986).* Rome: Citta Nuova Editrice, 1987, 11–14.

Lee, Patrick. "The Permanence of the Ten Commandments: St. Thomas and His Modern Commentators". *Theological Studies* 42 (1981), 422–33.

May, William E. "Making True Moral Judgments and Good Moral Choices", *Faith & Reason* 13 (1987), 283–99.

——. *Moral Absolutes: Catholic Tradition, Current Trends, and the Truth.* Milwaukee: Marquette University Press, 1989.

——. "The Natural Law and Objective Morality: A Thomistic Perspective". In *Principles of Catholic Moral Life,* edited by William E. May. Chicago: Franciscan Herald Press, 1981, 151–90.

Thomas Aquinas, *Summa Theologiae,* 1–2, qq. 90–94, q. 100; aa. 1, 3, 8, 11.

Vatican II. *Dignitatis Humanae,* nn. 2, 3, 14.

——. *Gaudium et Spes,* nn. 16, 17, 27, 35, 38, 39.

A RESPONSE TO DR. WILLIAM E. MAY

by Rev. Kevin Thomas McMahon, S.T.D.

INTRODUCTION

During the first few days of November 1988, it was my good
fortune to be a participant at an international meeting of moral
theologians held in Rome to commemorate the twentieth anniver-
sary of *Humanae Vitae*. At that meeting the encyclical was hailed
as a prophetic document for three basic reasons: its reaffirmation
of the Tradition's view on the meanings and purposes of human
sexuality; its reassertion of the moral truth regarding the genera-
tion of human life; and its warning against the intrinsic evil of
contraception and the moral evils that inevitably would flow
from the adoption of a contraceptive mentality.

To be sure, the position taken by the theologians who presented
papers there—including Professors May and Grisez—was not the
response one typically finds in the writings of many, perhaps even
a majority, of moral theologians. Theirs was not the response one
sees reported in the results of random opinion polls taken among
Catholics. Nor was it, and this gets us closer to our topic, the
reaction one receives from some bishops and priests.

What then could we say of that group of theologians? That
they were outdated—unaware of modern problems that place
couples in circumstances where the greater good is served only by
a willful violation of *Humanae Vitae*'s normative teaching? Should
they be discredited on the claim that invited participants represented
too one-sided a view? Should they be summarily dismissed as
"outside the mainstream" of contemporary moral thought? Perhaps even denounced (as they were in the Italian press and by
certain well-known moral theologians) as rigorists? Or should
they be taken seriously and their conclusions accepted?

The answer to all these questions is important, I believe, because although we address a different topic, this group is very similar to the one that met in Rome. The similarity extends beyond our respective agreement with the Church's moral teaching to the reasons for that agreement—reasons very carefully set forth in the paper just delivered.

A SHARED CONVICTION

In outlining natural-law theory as it was framed by Saint Thomas and recently reformulated by Germain Grisez, Dr. May points up a conviction forcibly put forth in the writings of both, namely, that there is a *moral truth*—a truth that generates not only those formal moral norms that govern the general requirements of the moral life, but also those specific moral norms that apply to every particular moral action. This truth is universal, precluding every form of subjectivism and relativism. It is eternal, precluding historical or cultural factors that would condition its validity. This truth is normative for all moral beings and does not only gradually become applicable.

Moreover, it is argued that the authority for what this truth demands is founded not simply in the *will* of some legislator who arbitrarily determines what is moral and immoral, making disobedience or the breaking of a law the definition of moral evil or sin; rather, the authority of this moral truth rests upon the intrinsic link between what it demands and the very nature of the person who exists and is fulfilled according to the perfectly wise and loving plan of God. By such an account moral goodness lies in fullness of being, while sin or moral evil is the self-mutilating introduction of privation by the person through his free choices.

Beyond this, it is maintained that knowledge of moral truth is accessible to all naturally through the use of reason—by appealing to that law written in our hearts. That because of human finitude and the consequences of original sin, errors in the judgment of conscience are possible when one relies on human reason alone.

That such errors, however, can be avoided by deferring to the certain expression of moral truth given in divine revelation found in Sacred Scripture and in the living Tradition of the Church. That through its teaching office, the Church articulates the moral truth that it has come to know both through natural law and divine revelation. And, that this truth that it passes on to all is protected from error by the gift of the Holy Spirit and the charism of office to discern the movement of that Spirit in the life of the community.

This conviction presented by Drs. May and Grisez strikes a harmonious chord with Fr. Vanhoye's discussion of the relation between "the law" and "life in Christ" found in the writings of Saint Paul; and with the ecclesiological and ministerial reflections offered by Fr. Chantraine. One can rightly conclude that this is a shared conviction; one can rightly conclude, I believe, that this is the faith of the Church.

PASTORAL PRACTICE OF PRIESTS

It was on the basis of this shared conviction that the speakers described a particular view of the priest as moral teacher and guide. That is, he would know and accept this moral truth, and out of love for those to whom he ministers—out of concern for their true fulfillment—he would instruct them in this truth, helping them form their consciences correctly. By his example and spiritual support he would encourage them to live according to true judgments of conscience.

It is here that we are able to introduce a question that may help further our reflection on the Catholic priest as moral teacher and guide. And so we ask, Can one really expect that priests do accept this moral truth, that they do pass it on in their instructions, and that they even consider themselves called to live according to its demands? This question may seem radically unfair and totally off the mark. Nevertheless, the reality in many parts of the world is that many priests have learned a different moral methodology—one that assigns a more limited role to moral truth; one that allows no absolutes with regard to specific moral norms; one, in fact, that encourages the violation of many specific moral norms held and taught by the Church. Simply put, many priests are thoroughly proportionalistic in their moral methodology and, consequently, in their approach to pastoral practice.

What if one were to gauge the influence of proportionalism and theological dissent on the pastoral practices of priests by examining the opinion polls conducted by the media among "Catholics" to whom they minister? One would have to accept that many are indeed *schooled* in ignoring or violating Catholic moral teaching, claiming justification for doing so in the right to follow conscience. In making this claim, one should note, however, that there is no notion that the judgment of conscience could be erroneous; there is no notion that the violations of moral truth are injurious to the violators; there is no notion that they should repent and change their hearts in this matter. But why is this so? Does everything not at least point to a lack of belief in the existence of an eternal and universal moral truth, by which they are to form their consciences and live their lives if they are to grow in holiness and reach the fulfillment to which they are called?

It is true that one could point to many other possible causes for the present state of affairs. One could blame the many misinterpretations of the Second Vatican Council; one could suggest that the laity is more educated than in former times and much less likely to accept teachings that their culturally conditioned practical wits lead them to reject. One could suggest that the lack of unity among bishops on moral matters is to blame, or that it is simply ignorance or intimidation that forces some ministers—bishops and priests—to shrink from teaching the moral truth.

I will not minimize the importance of these possible factors, but it seems clear that the role of the Catholic priest as moral teacher and guide is fundamentally rooted in his response to certain questions. Does he believe that there is a moral truth possessing the characteristics detailed by Drs. May and Grisez? Does he believe that it is this truth that is held and taught by the Church? Does he believe that moral truth can be applied to specific moral actions and be absolutely binding in certain instances?

Despite the obstacles to the mission of the Church represented in the pastoral ministries of those who offer a negative response to these questions, I would like to conclude on a positive note. For there can be no doubt that the voice of the Magisterium and the pastoral practice of what I would like to believe is the vast majority of priests assures us of this fact: that the perfectly wise and loving plan of God, from which all moral teaching derives its reasonableness and normativity, continues to be clearly spoken through the Church of Christ. Whatever the state of the present moral crisis, hope abounds in the promise of Christ to be with us always.

LEGALISM, MORAL TRUTH
AND PASTORAL PRACTICE

I. WHAT IS LEGALISM AND WHY IS IT WIDESPREAD?

Legalism is the view that moral norms are like positive laws, rules that depend on someone's free choice. Given a legalistic view of moral norms, both their obligatoriness and that of positive laws, which presupposes morality, seem to flow from the lawgiver's will rather than from intelligible requirements of a wise plan for realizing the good.

Christian legalists reduce moral obligation to God's law, understood as a set of precepts that the Almighty adopts and imposes. Some have thought that God could even have obliged us to hate him. Most legalists have held, more plausibly, that actions can be more or less suitable to human nature, and that God creates moral obligations by requiring certain suitable actions and by forbidding certain unsuitable ones. In this view, God's legislative will transforms into virtuous deeds and sins what otherwise would only be manifestations of good and bad judgment.

Legal systems typically include a presumption in favor of liberty: what is not forbidden is permitted, and doubtful laws do not bind. Consequently, legalism suggests that we are generally free to do as we please, that moral obligations limit this freedom, and that we need not accept this limitation unless an obligation is clear. From this follows the legalistic view that one can do no wrong if one follows one's conscience.

Human lawmakers attach penalties to laws to motivate obedience.

Because the penalties for disobedience are not inherent consequences of wrongful acts, the authorities can impose, mitigate or forego the penalties for policy reasons or as their wrath or clemency moves them. Legalists think a higher power similarly backs up morality with attached sanctions. Christian legalists think of heaven and hell as the reward for obedience and punishment for disobedience that God attaches to his law.

Only manifest transgressions of positive laws are punishable. Minimum fulfillment of a law does not break it. So in a legalistic view of morality, it seems unnecessary to commit oneself to pursuing the goods and avoiding the evils to which moral norms point. One need only avoid disobedience. Therefore, legalists are minimalists. Also, those who are invincibly ignorant of a law cannot disobey it with criminal intent. Therefore, legalists think that, other things being equal, wrongdoing through ignorance is preferable to disobedience, and that it often is best to leave people in good faith.

The preceding sketch describes what legalism is. But to understand it fully, one must see why it is so widespread.

Children initially cannot grasp the reasons behind any of the norms with which adults confront them. At first all norms seem alike. Inevitably, children think that the important thing about any norm is that adults want it obeyed. Thus, as children become aware of moral obligations, they regard them legalistically. This mentality is confirmed when parents reinforce moral norms by rewarding good behavior and punishing naughtiness. Even adults tend to think that moral norms receive their directive force from some authority's will.

For believers, additional factors are at work. The Old Testament lends itself to a legalistic reading. Genesis makes it clear that like everything else apart from God, morality would not exist had he not freely created. And Israel hands on moral precepts as the nucleus of her God-given law. But Israel is a theocratic polity, and so her code necessarily embraces morality and also commingles with it all her positive law. Accordingly, it is easy for readers of the Old Testament to confuse morality with positive law, and to suppose that both depend on God in the same way.

Then, too, because Israel's hopes are this-worldly and national-istic, righteousness and sinfulness are not intrinsically related to the realization and frustration of those hopes. The carrying out of the blessings and curses attached to Israel's law, including its moral precepts, seems to depend on God much as the carrying out of rewards and punishments attached to human law depends on public authorities.

Moreover, because God is the one Lord of all creation, evil in the world cannot be reduced to conflict among many gods or to an evil first principle opposed to God. Rather, God's plan seems to include the destruction of Israel's enemies as a means to her flourishing. Consequently, evil and good, death and life seem to flow from God's will in the same way. It readily appears that even the moral discriminations in God's law depend on his will rather than on his wisdom.

Christian moral instruction conveys the sound moral content of the Old Law but often retains its legalistic tendencies. So the first explanation of morality that Christian children are likely to hear is that some of the rules that adults impose are God's commands, and that God eventually will reward obedience and punish disobedience. While that explanation has a true sense, it also tends to confirm children's natural legalism. They are likely to grow up thinking that God could have prevented all sins: he need only have refrained from commanding people to do hard things and not to do enjoyable things.

An additional factor inclines Catholics to legalism. Traditional moral theology clarified many sharp but subtle distinctions—for example, between accepting death as Jesus did and committing suicide in a good cause, between justifiable military actions and the killing of noncombatants, and between the upright practice of natural family planning and contraception. To those who do not understand the reasons for such distinctions, they seem like the bright but somewhat arbitrary lines that human lawmakers often draw—for example, fornication with a consenting fifteen-year-old girl is rape, but with a sixteen-year-old it is not a crime; driving with one-tenths of 1 percent of alcohol in one's blood is a serious offense while driving with slightly less is not; and so on. The result is that Catholic moral teaching, by its use of the sharp distinctions that moral theology has clarified, inevitably looks, even to the faithful who are less well instructed, like a human legal system. And secular commentators, whose world view affords no insight into the bases of those moral norms that the Church teaches but the contemporary world rejects, naturally think that popes and bishops are not teachers but lawmakers: "Vatican bans in vitro fertilization!" and "Bishops bar use of condoms to prevent AIDS!" Hearing what the Church teaches from the mass media, the faithful absorb legalism along with the morning and evening news.

Last, but not least, legalism appeals to sinful human beings. Even if one breaks the rules, one still can hope to escape punishment because the offense may be forgiven and the deserved punishment remitted. Anyway, if sinning is mere rule breaking, it is not inherently foolish and deadly. And if moral norms are laws, most of one's life is not touched by them, and one generally is free to do as he pleases. Of course, one's freedom in a few matters is limited, but one often can find a way to do as he pleases without grossly transgressing moral limits. And if one obeys the rules, he can be sure that he is good. Even an occasional lapse cannot spoil a generally good record.

Such legalism corrupted the pharisaism that Jesus denounced. His criticism of certain Pharisees was not only that they were rigorists; he also condemned their moral evasiveness and laxism. Jesus rejected their whole legalistic view and the pastoral practice that went with it.

II. HOW ARE MORAL NORMS
CORRECTLY UNDERSTOOD AS TRUTHS?

The Old Testament offers some starting points for a nonlegalistic view of morality. God's will is creative; it brings creatures into existence and moves them toward their fulfillment. God does not make death, for he makes only what is good. Death is a punishment for sin, but sinners bring it upon themselves. God's plan of salvation extends beyond Israel to the nations; his love for some people does not entail hatred toward others. God wills good to all. He orders all things wisely and lovingly. Thus, his law is not a burdensome imposition but a blessing, a light on one's path. To ignore God's direction is foolish and self-destructive, while to follow it is fulfilling. Moral goodness begins with reverence toward God and love of neighbor. Morality is not primarily a matter of outward conformity to law but a matter of the heart. Therefore, when sinners repent, God heals the self-mutilation that their sins caused by creating new hearts in them.

God's revelation in Jesus unfolds these beginnings. Jesus reveals that God is a communion of three persons, distinct from one another but perfectly one in love, and that God calls us to share in divine communion and to live in familial companionship with one another. God's love is a gift, but each one who accepts this gift can abide in it and work toward the ideal of loving God with his whole mind, heart, soul and strength. The command to do this directs God's little children to be like their heavenly Father. The command to love one's neighbor as oneself, in communion with God, directs God's children to treat one another and themselves in accord with the reality of the divine–human communion—the kingdom—into which they are called.

Because of sin, wayward emotions are a law in one's members that tempt one not to follow moral truth, the law in one's mind. Thus, sinners experience moral norms as impositions because these norms express demands that unfettered reason makes on wayward feelings. Although doing what is morally good is reasonable and humanly fulfilling, it often seems foolish and inhumanly difficult. But those motivated by love, who live by the Spirit, do not experience moral truth as an imposed law. The law of the Spirit of life in Jesus frees them from such slavery (cf. Rm 8:2).

These revealed data provided Christian reflection with material for a nonlegalistic view of morality and of the foundations of law. Saint Thomas brought this reflection to a splendid synthesis in his treatise on law in his *Summa Theologiae*. Law is a directive of practical reason. God is sovereignly free in choosing to create; but eternal law, his plan for creating and governing creation, flows from his wisdom and goodness. Eternal law is the foundation of all other law, and its binding force and that of all other law, including positive law, depend on the law's intelligible relationship to the good toward which it directs action, not on the lawgiver's will.

Since God made humankind in his own image, he equips us from the start with some knowledge of his plan—"natural law"—so that we spontaneously understand practical principles that point us toward the goods fulfilling us as individuals and communities. All moral norms flow from natural law, and so the whole moral content of the Old Law also is written in our hearts. Because natural law directs us to what will truly fulfill us, God, given that he has made us what we are, has no choice about the content of morality. God is free and all-powerful, but even he cannot make black to be white, what is humanly destructive to be humanly fulfilling. Therefore, God commands us to act only in morally good ways, not because he wants to impose anything, but because, loving us, he wants us to do what is for our own good.

On this basis, one can provide a nonlegalistic account of all the moral requirements of Christian life. God's love embraces all peoples; his mercy extends to the wicked as well as to the righteous. Even toward the wicked God wills only good. He does not will but only permits evil, sin and its consequences. Thus, evil is centered in alienation from God and the inevitable consequences of that alienation, and must be understood as the privation of good rather than as the positive contrary of good. So God's redemptive work in Jesus neither segregates and excludes nor attacks and destroys what sin damaged, but calls it back and restores it by means of healing love.

Because Christians share in this redemptive work, specific moral requirements logically follow. They are to be perfect as their heavenly Father is perfect, and so they are to will only good, even to enemies, as God himself does. They must spread the gospel and bear witness to it, even to death, imitate God's mercy and build up his kingdom by forgiveness and beneficence toward those in need, and live chastely as members of Jesus' body in which the Spirit dwells. The New Testament also makes it clear that the morality already contained in the Old Law is not arbitrary but is a necessary consequence of love, for love fulfills the law. For instance, if one loves his neighbors as God loves them, he cannot choose to kill even an enemy or to replace even an unfaithful spouse.

God initially creates us with unfulfilled potentialities so that we can help create ourselves, and in that way be more like him than if he created us from the start with greater perfection. To enable us to be like himself and to cooperate in his work, God gives us freedom of choice. Thus, in this world, God continues to create us through our own choices and acts.

Seriously evil choices and acts are self-determining. Mortal sins last unless one repents. In and of themselves, unrepented mortal sins exclude one from the kingdom because such sins constitute a self incompatible with love. For example, Jesus warns that those who refuse to meet others' urgent needs "will go away into eternal punishment" (Mt 25:46). This is not a threat that Jesus will impose punishment on the uncharitable; it is simply a clarification of the fact that refusal to act as a member of Christ toward his other members is incompatible with sharing in the communion of divine family life. The First Letter of John makes this clear: "If anyone has the world's goods and sees his brother in need, yet closes his heart against him, how does God's love abide in him?" (1 Jn 3:17).

Not only sins but also upright choices and acts are self-determining. Still, the relationship of sins to hell and of good deeds to heaven is not symmetrical. God warns of hell because sinners can consign themselves to it despite everything he does to save them. But God gratuitously promises heaven, and Christians must hope in him for it. For only God can overcome sin and death and create the new heavens and new earth. Nevertheless, what one does in this life lasts. Charity and its fruits will endure in the kingdom. Indeed, as Vatican II teaches, in heaven all the good fruits of human nature and effort will find a place, cleansed of sin and perfected.[1] Thus, the greatest significance of morally good choices and acts is that they build up persons, interpersonal relationships and a humanized world that God will transform into his kingdom.

It follows that morality extends to one's whole life. It should be a life of faith in Jesus, and whatever one does should be done in his name. Love, the law of the Spirit, embraces every good and resists every evil. Because his entire life should respond to God's calling, one never is free to do as he pleases, except insofar as he becomes like Jesus, for whom acting according to love, doing the Father's will, was his bread and wine.

III. HOW HAS LEGALISM AFFECTED PASTORAL PRACTICE?

Even before the current moral crisis in the Church, legalism affected pastoral practice in many ways.

Very often God's sovereignty and the Church's teaching authority tended to overshadow the inherent reasonableness of moral requirements and their intrinsic relationship to the kingdom. Obedience rather than charity seemed to be the basic Christian virtue. Hell was a punishment that God would impose rather than the inevitable outcome of unrepented mortal sin.

Many pastors stressed the minimum required to avoid mortal sin. Insofar as most of the life of a layperson is taken up with

---

[1] *Gaudium et Spes,* no. 39.

secular concerns, the positive content of the laity's lives seemed to have little religious significance. Thus, many Catholics thought that holiness is reserved for the clergy and religious. Pastors and teachers usually assumed that a few young people had vocations, but that most did not. Marriage, work, and so on were not regarded as possible elements of a Christian vocation and often were treated as no more than so many fields mined with temptations.

Because invincible ignorance frees one from guilt, pastors were more concerned about the sincerity of penitents than about the correctness of their consciences. Considering morality a matter of laws rather than of truths, pastors assumed that people could easily be in good faith while doing what is objectively wrong. And ignoring the phenomena of rationalization and self-deception, pastors confidently thought that they could discern when penitents were and were not in good faith.

During the twentieth century, pastoral treatment of repetitious sins through weakness—especially masturbation, homosexual behavior, premarital sex play and contraception within marriage—grew increasingly mild. Pastors correctly recognized that weakness and immaturity can lessen such sins' malice. Thinking legalistically, they did not pay enough attention to the sins' inherent badness and harmfulness, and they developed the idea that people can freely choose to do something that they regard as a grave matter without committing a mortal sin. This idea presupposes that in making choices people are not responsible precisely for choosing what they choose. That presupposition makes sense within a legalistic framework, because lawgivers can take into account mitigating factors and limit legal culpability. But it makes no sense for morality correctly understood, because moral responsibility in itself is not something attached to moral acts but simply is moral agents' self-determination in making free choices.

Repetitious sinners through weakness also were handicapped by their own legalism. Not seeing the inherent badness of their sins, they felt that they were only violating inscrutable rules. When temptation grew strong, they had little motive to resist, especially because they could easily go to confession and have the violation fixed. Beginning on Saturday they were holy; by Friday they were again sinners. This cyclic sanctity robbed many people's lives of Christian dynamism and contributed to the dry rot in the Church that became manifest in the 1960s, when the waves of sexual permissiveness battered her.

Theologians and pastors who dissent from received Catholic teaching think they are rejecting legalism because they set aside what they think are mere rules in favor of what they feel are more reasonable standards. Their views are thoroughly imbued with legalism, however. For dissenters think of valid moral norms as rules formulated to protect relevant values. Some even make their legalism explicit by denying that there is any necessary connection between moral goodness (which they restrict to the transcendental level of a love with no specific content) and right action (which they isolate at the categorical level of inner-worldly behavior). But whether their legalism is explicit or not, all the dissenters hold that specific moral norms admit exceptions whenever, all things considered, making an exception seems the best—or least bad—thing to do. Most dissenters also think that specific moral norms that were valid in times past can be inappropriate today, and so they regard the Church's contested moral teachings as outdated rules that the Church should change.

Dissenters also assume that doubtful laws do not bind, and so they think that the Church's moral teaching is not binding unless the case for it puts it beyond doubt. The contested norms plainly are doubted; many people say they experience no ill effects when they disobey them, and many theologians reject them. In other words, what is doubted can be doubted, and what can be doubted is doubtful. Thus, dissenters conclude, experience proves that the contested norms are doubtful and no longer binding. Of course, these norms remain the Church's "official" teaching. But dissenters regard them as they do other laws that remain on the books, although experience has shown them to be unworkable, so that the authorities no longer try to enforce them and the public ignores them.

Dissenters also feel pastorally justified because dissent lessens the burden on the faithful by encouraging them to follow their own consciences against the Church's teaching. Conceiving conscience legalistically and disregarding the possibility that the norms they contest might be truths, dissenters do not consider whether they might be encouraging self-deception, obduracy in sin and presumption. Rather, they think that those who insist on received moral teachings impose unnecessary guilt on people, and that pastoral prudence demands that this guilt be relieved.

Legalism also remains prevalent in the thinking and practice of many theologians and pastors who loyally affirm the Church's moral teachings. Legalistic loyalists not only prolong preconciliar legalism, but also respond to the moral crisis in the Church in a characteristically legalistic way. They consider it most important that the faithful not rebel against the Church's authority. So, rather than working to understand the teaching and make it understandable to the faithful, rather than figuring out how to put the teaching into practice and helping the faithful to do that, they look for ways—some of which overlap with the approaches of dissenting theologians—to reconcile contrary practice with docility to the Church.

Some legalistic loyalists explain that if one tries to understand the Church's teaching but cannot, he may follow his own conscience, provided that he remains prepared to obey should the Church ever make it clear that he must. Some apply theories of fundamental option that, whatever their nuances, in practice assure the faithful that if their moral record is generally good, sexual sins through weakness will not count against them. Some characterize the contested teachings as ideals, thus legalistically suggesting that one need not regard them as strict rules. And many adopt a pastoral policy of gradualism, according to which those who accept a norm in theory and take even the smallest step toward putting it into practice have done the minimum necessary to avoid mortal sin.

Jones, a good small-town police officer, knows the local people and overlooks some of their law breaking: an elderly couple making home brew for themselves and a few friends, an unemployed man hunting out of season to feed his family, and so on. When a fight occurs in the pub and the place is smashed up, Officer Jones charges nobody with assault but makes sure that those responsible repair the damage. Catching boys stealing from the hardware store, Jones delivers them to their fathers for a thrashing. Similarly, for legalists, a good pastor is a moderate and gentle administrator of the moral law. He knows when to close his eyes and when to give dispensations from the moral rules. He realizes that many people simply cannot live up to the strict requirements of morality.

Pastors should strive to overcome every vestige of legalism in their minds and hearts. If they do, they will not try to be moderate and gentle administrators of moral law. Will they become neurotic enforcers, imitating Captain Queeg rather than Officer Jones? No. Martinets also are legalists. If pastors escape postconciliar legalism, they need not revert to preconciliar legalism. Instead, free of legalism, they can imitate Jesus. He proceeded like a good physician who teaches people to distinguish being healthy from feeling well, stresses preventive medicine, helps the sick and injured to regain health, and never prescribes painkillers to those who would use them to avoid life-saving surgery.

Setting aside analogies, one can articulate the principle of pastoral practice without legalism: pastors free of legalism will work to understand in the light of faith the deepest reasons that it is good to be good and the specific reasons that each moral norm is true. They will teach this body of moral truth to the faithful and help them in every way possible to put it into practice.

Having stated the general principle for pastoral renewal, one can sketch out some of its specific features.

Nonlegalistic moral preaching and teaching will fittingly begin with the Holy Trinity, with the divine-human communion to which they call us, with Jesus who mediates that communion. The heavenly kingdom is God's family; one is blessed to be a member of it. For in it life has meaning and hope is secure. This starting point makes it clear why one should abide in God's love and why one should love neighbors, even enemies, as oneself.

Pastors free of legalism will explain how good actions are grounded in love and are inherently related to human well-being. They will emphasize that every good action in this life provides material for the kingdom, so that every action has everlasting significance. They will teach that every Christian should live an apostolic life and so should make daily life into rational worship, offered with Jesus' sacrifice in the Mass. They will help each member of their flocks to find his personal vocation, to commit himself to it, and to fulfill it every day of his life.

Such pastors also will explain how bad actions are contrary to love or, at least, are incompatible with its perfection, and how they are inherently related to human misery and diminishment. They will make it clear that because moral norms are the truth about the good that human persons can choose and do, choices at odds with them, even if they are made through invincible ignorance, are really bad. They will explain how such objectively wrong acts detract from the well-being of persons both as individuals and as a community, and provide poorer material for the kingdom than good choices and actions would provide. They will emphasize that love therefore requires that one energetically seek moral truth.

When such pastors preach or teach about any specific norm, they will avoid even true statements that are likely to be misunderstood and taken in a legalistic sense. For example, they will not say that the norm should be obeyed because it is the law of God nor that Catholics must accept it because the Church authoritatively teaches it. Instead, they will point out that because God is a wise and loving Father, one can be sure that his commands direct his children to what is good for them, and that because Jesus teaches in his Church, Catholics can be confident that her teaching is true.

Pastors free of legalism will help their flocks see why Christians must be different. People without faith understandably try to segregate evil or to overcome it with force and, when all else fails, compromise with it to make the best of this sinful world. When Christians confront evil, they should make the sharp but subtle distinctions that moral truth requires, and they must, of course, avoid sin and resist injustice as love demands. But they may never betray love by choosing evil so that good may come about. Instead, following Jesus, they must draw close to sinners and the misery that results from sin, accept the suffering that evil inflicts, and work to overcome evil with healing love, but never forget that only God can transform this fallen world into the new Jerusalem.

Such pastors will assure the faithful that God loves them unconditionally; that, like the prodigal's father, he loves them even when they sin; indeed, that God loves even the damned — they would cease to exist if he did not love them. But pastors will explain that being loved by God is not enough to be in friendship with him, because friendship is mutual love. They will exhort the faithful, as Jesus did, to accept God's mercy, repent their sins and abide in love. But they also will warn, as Jesus did, that hell awaits those who do not abide in love. And they will correct the mistake of legalists who confuse this warning with a threat. When one calls children's attention to a dead animal in the road — "That young deer didn't look before running out" — one is not threatening to run over them if they cross the highway carelessly. The penalty for their carelessness will not be something one would impose or could prevent. So too God and hell.

Pastors free of legalism will teach the faithful how sin makes moral requirements seem to be alien impositions, help them see through this illusion, and encourage them to look forward to and experience the freedom of God's children, who rejoice in the fruit of the Spirit and no longer experience the constraint of law.

They will explain that while one sometimes must choose contrary to positive laws and cannot always meet their requirements, one always can choose in truth and abide in love. They will acknowledge the paradox of freedom—that we seem unable to resist freely choosing to sin—the paradox that Saint Paul neatly formulates: "I do not understand my own actions. For I do not do what I want, but I do the very thing I hate" (Rm 7:15). But they also will proclaim the liberating power of grace, and help the faithful learn by experience that when one comes to understand the inherent evil of sin and intrinsic beauty of goodness, enjoys the support of a community of faith whose members bear one another's burdens, begs God for his help, and confidently expects it, then the Spirit of him who raised Jesus from the dead raises him from his sins, and he discovers that with the Spirit's grace one can consistently resist sin and choose life.

Such a pastor also will work hard in practical ways to help his people overcome obstacles to living holy lives. If he finds that some are tempted to sin because they do not know virtuous ways to solve their problems, he will encourage those capable of it to develop and disseminate the relevant knowledge—as did the pastors who fostered the work of Knaus, Billings and others in natural family planning. If he finds that people are tempted to sin because of poverty, he will do what he can to help them and will encourage others to do the works of justice and mercy that will alleviate their pressing needs—as many pastors have done. And he will never let his flock forget that Christians love one another effectively by bearing one another's burdens, helping one another to avoid sin and its occasions, and encouraging one another to fulfill their personal vocations.

Finally, pastors free of legalism will teach people that conscience is nothing but one's final judgment as to what he should do and not do; that one's first responsibility is to do his best to make sure that this judgment is true; that the Church's teaching hands on the moral truth that Jesus exemplified and taught; that self-deception can make one feel sure that a sin is permissible without freeing him from guilt for committing it, that doing what is wrong because of a blamelessly mistaken conscience always causes harm and often leads to tragedy; and that in every situation one should pray for the Holy Spirit's help to see what is good and holy, rather than try to discern the minimum necessary to avoid mortal sin. Only then will pastors add that one must follow his conscience—of course, one must follow it—against his own contrary inclinations, social pressures and human laws that demand that he act against the moral truth that faith teaches, and so forth.

The following is a sketch of an answer to the objection "What do these laymen know about pastoral practice? If they heard a few confessions, they would find out in short order that their ideas are totally unrealistic."

First, some norms of pastoral practice are technical; they concern the ways and means of doing what priests should do. It does take experience to develop and apply such norms; however, the more important norms of pastoral practice are not technical. These determine, not ways and means, but precisely what pastors should do and not do. One can call these nontechnical norms "constitutive".

These constitutive norms follow from basic moral principles and from what the Gospel tells us about Christian life and priestly ministry. Anyone who knows these sources can derive the constitutive norms without having experience in pastoral work. To deny this would be to assume that experience can revise moral principles or the Gospel itself. Of course, some today make that assumption, but their theories logically point to ethical relativism and the rejection of the Catholic conception of divine revelation.

Second, over the years the laity experience the good and bad practices of many pastors and see the good and evil effects of pastoral practice in the lives of their loved ones. Then, too, many priests share their experience with lay scholars. Furthermore, all of us are experiencing what surely is a pastoral disaster: most Catholics have virtually abandoned the sacrament of penance. Even Catholics who are still trying to live up to the Church's moral teaching apparently do not experience enough benefit from the sacrament of penance to be motivated to receive it regularly.

Third, homogeneous groups with common responsibilities and experiences also share common temptations and develop a common mentality, which always is somewhat biased. That is true even of Catholic priests. So a lay theologian is uniquely situated to look at the priestly ministry objectively and to criticize pastoral practice.

This threefold answer to the objection "What does a layman know about pastoral practice?" exactly parallels the answer priests have given to the challenge "What do you clerics know about marriage and family life?" Priests always rightly pointed out that the relevant norms are moral truths that follow from principles of natural law and the Gospel, that a priest enjoys the experience of his family of origin and of the many faithful with whom he has dealt, and that his own celibate life enables him to see the objective truth about marriage and family life more clearly than do those who are living that life and struggling with its temptations.

A RESPONSE TO DR. GERMAIN GRISEZ

by Dr. J. Brian Benestad

In reading Professor Grisez's paper I repeatedly asked myself what's behind legalism and the failure of many pastors to promote the renewal of moral life. In Section III of his paper, Professor Grisez promises to explain how legalism affected pastoral practice even before the current moral crisis in the Church. In fact, his thought-provoking observations begin to explain not only how but also why legalism has become an even greater problem in the Catholic Church since the end of the Second Vatican Council. In addition, Professor Grisez's readers might be led to conclude that legalism is a symptom of even more fundamental problems in the moral understanding of Catholic pastors and theologians.

Here are Grisez's eight or so manifestations or causes of legalism, partially restated at times in order to draw out the implications or possible implications of the text:

1. Pastors very often failed to see the inherent reasonableness or goodness of God's requirements and the inherent badness and harmfulness of sin. So, for example, hell was a punishment that God would impose rather than the inevitable outcome of unrepented mortal sin.

2. Pastors stressed the minimum or negative commandments rather than positive attitudes and actions or the virtue that leads people to be inventive in their love of God and neighbor. Urgent longings to love more deeply burn away vices, to use Saint Augustine's expression.

3. Pastors placed too much stress on sincerity and not enough on a correctly formed conscience, and failed to perceive rationalization or self-deception in penitents.

4. Dissenting theologians and pastors deny any necessary connection between moral goodness and right action. This denial probably has its roots in utilitarian philosophy. In

addition, disassociating moral goodness from right action offends common sense.

5. Dissenting theologians and pastors teach that there are exceptions to all specific or material moral norms.

6. Dissenting theologians and pastors teach that experience is a *locus theologicus.* Experience proves that contested moral norms may not be true and therefore, being doubtful, cannot bind.

7. Carving out exceptions to norms, dissenters believe, shows compassion by lightening burdens on the faithful.

8. Legalistic loyalists, including theologians and pastors, undermine the will of the faithful to strive for perfection by seeking the truth and living in conformity with its full requirements.

In the measure that Professor Grisez's analysis is correct, pastors will be seriously hindered not only in their pastoral ministry, but also in their own pursuit of holiness.

Grisez's eight manifestations or causes of legalism could simply be described as signs or causes of the contemporary moral crisis in the Catholic Church. I would also add some other ways in which theology has contributed to deficient pastoral practice: by denying the Church's ability to make binding pronouncements on specific moral issues; by separating faith from morality and claiming that there is no such thing as a specific Christian morality (as if morality is not decisively affected by the Creed, the sacraments and the Lord's Prayer. In other words, all morality, in principle, is simply human morality accessible to anyone who can use his reason); by not effectively linking rights to duties or virtue; and by using fundamental moral theology principally as an instrument to determine the proper exceptions to negative moral precepts, thereby neglecting the principal spiritual and moral problems of Catholics and the rest of humanity. Several other factors contributing to deficient pastoral practice are the decline of the love of learning among the clergy and the practice of assiduous study; the failure of clergy and laity to pass on the faith to so many young people; the lack of courage in both the clergy and laity to oppose the *Zeitgeist;* and the breakup of the family.

The very root of the moral crisis in the Church is the prevalence of a historicist mode of thinking. According to historicism, all principles of justice are mutable; all thought is historically conditioned. Nature as norm of human conduct is rejected; what essentially constitutes man is basically changeable. In the words of the political philosopher Leo Strauss, "Whereas, according to the ancients, philosophizing means to leave the cave, according to our contemporaries all philosophizing essentially belongs to a 'historical world', 'culture', 'civilization', *'Weltanschauung',* that is, to what Plato had called the cave. We shall call this view 'historicism' ".[1] Catholic revisionist theologians prefer the term *historical consciousness* to historicism. They describe historical consciousness as the "hallmark of modernity". The shift from classical to historical consciousness is sometimes described as irreversible. In a very famous article Joseph Fuchs, S.J. describes the effect of historical consciousness on the interpretation and applicability of moral norms in Scripture:

> The moral behavioral norms in Scripture are directed to actual persons of a definite era and culture. Hence, their character of absoluteness would not signify primarily universality but objectivity, and the latter can denote either the objectively right evaluation in a particular culturally conditioned human situation or necessary conformity to the moral views of the morally elite in a given society.[2]

In this perspective, historicism does not make morality arbitrary, but relative to a particular age or particular situation. Proponents of this view would deny that this is relativism or situation ethics or utilitarianism. Taking account of historical

---

[1] Leo Strauss, *Natural Right and History* (Chicago: University of Chicago Press, 1953), 12.

[2] Joseph Fuchs, S.J., "The Absoluteness of Moral Norms", in *Readings in Moral Theology,* no. 1, ed. Charles E. Curran and Richard A. McCormack, S.J. (New York: Paulist Press, 1979), 100.

consciousness is being attuned to the way things are. Historicist theologians could even argue that taking one's bearing by reality is the essential command of morality traditionally understood. There may even arise absolutes from the needs of a particular age or situation.

Acceptance of historicism as an absolute largely explains the following characteristics of theology today: rejection of nature as a norm, especially visible in the area of sexual morality; rejection of Aquinas' natural-law teaching; the effective denial of the Magisterium's authority in the area of specific moral norms; the failure to accept the inherent goodness or badness of human attitudes and actions; the focus on exceptions to negative moral commandments; the stress on the role of experience and inductive methodologies that gather data; the focus on sincerity or commitment as a substitute for struggling to understand the way things are by reason and faith; the denial of a specific Christian morality; the sense of justification in desiring to be more or less independent of the authority of Scripture, Tradition and the Church; the desire to be in the mainstream of American culture; the loss of belief in the power of reason and faith to transcend one's culture.

Historicism also partly explains the substitution of political reform for moral conversion and the stress on rights rather than virtue and the common good, as well as the eruption of out-and-out relativism. Finally, because of historicist influences, faith and reason are severely hindered in dealing with the perennial causes of moral crisis, viz., love of pleasure, wealth, praise, honor and power. And because of the pervasiveness of historicism, there is also a lack of incentive to seek out wisdom in the great authors of the past.

The fourth section of Professor Grisez's paper, on the renewal of moral practice, discusses essential ingredients of the solution to the moral crisis. Professor Grisez rightly observes that pastors must "work to understand in the light of faith the deepest reasons that it is good to be good and the specific reasons that each moral norm is true". In addition, a pastor must help the faithful put Catholic moral teaching into practice in every aspect of their lives. In the rest of his paper, Professor Grisez goes on to sketch out some specific features of his general principle for pastoral renewal. For example, following a blamelessly mistaken conscience "always causes harm and often leads to tragedy". It is especially important these days for the Church to stress that sincerity and good intentions are not enough; the Church must focus on the truth. Today the neglect of the body in the name of physicalism or biologism reinforces the emphasis on autonomy and the reshaping of reality by one's sincere will. In the words of Dr. Leon Kass:

> [I]n ethics ... theorists of personhood, consciousness, and autonomy ... treat the essential human being as pure will and reason, as if bodily life counted for nothing, or did not even exist.[3]

While Professor Grisez suggests that dissenting theology has had a bad influence on pastoral practice, he does not see fit in this last section on pastoral renewal to discuss the *educational* implications of his suggestions for pastoral practice. In my mind, many pastors will not be able to do what Professor Grisez proposes unless they receive not only spiritual training but also a liberal education, especially one including a sound philosophical and theological formation, which, unfortunately, is neither widely appreciated nor even readily available. The leading pastors, i.e., bishops, as well as theologians and philosophers in the universities and seminaries, have joint responsibility for improving the education of today's priests. When a seminarian receives a poor philosophical education and an exclusive diet of revisionist moral theology, he usually will not be in a position to act as a moral guide for the faithful. Without a better education, revisionist theologians themselves will not be able to see the deficiencies and radical incompleteness of their approach to moral matters. The study of philosophy helped Saint Augustine free himself from his life-threatening errors. It was the study of Cicero's *Exhortation to Philosophy* at the age of nineteen that instilled in him an undying love of learning.

[3] Leon Kass, *Toward a More Natural Science: Biology and Human Affairs* (New York: The Free Press, 1985), 277.

CONCLUSION

The liberal education of priests in moral matters must deal with all
that pertains to living a moral life — to life in the trenches, as one
of my colleagues puts it. A careful study of many classic Christian
and non-Christian texts could help seminarians develop into good
moral teachers and guides. For example, reading Georges Bernanos'
Diary of a Country Priest and Alessandro Manzoni's *The Bethrothed*
or *I Promessi Sposi* will help candidates for the priesthood understand the nature of virtue and vice as well as the wide-ranging
impact of their own virtues and vices. Both Bernanos, the twentieth-
century French novelist, and Manzoni, the nineteenth-century
Italian novelist — virtually unknown in the United States — present
moving pictures of good priests who have the insight and courage
to help people overcome sin in their lives. Manzoni shows how
the attitudes of an intimidated priest adversely affect the lives of
people in his charge. Bernanos also presents inspiring images of
God's grace and human receptivity.

Even Plato takes us beyond the narrow confines of moral
disputes today. In the *Laws* he identifies the following as fit
subject matter for the laws of the polis:

> In all their mingling with one another one must keep
> a guard, watching their pains and pleasures, their desires and
> the ardor of all their erotic longings, blaming and praising
> correctly by means of the laws themselves. Moreover, in fits
> of anger, in fears, in the disturbances that come over souls
> in bad fortune and the release from such things that comes
> with good fortune, in the experience brought by diseases and
> wars and poverty, and the experiences brought upon human
> beings by the opposite circumstances — in all such situations
> what is noble and ignoble in each case must be taught and
> defined.[4]

---

[4] Plato, *The Laws of Plato,* trans. by Thomas L. Pangle (New York: Basic Books,
1980), 632a–b, 10–11.

While the laws in a liberal democracy cannot exercise the role of Plato's laws, moral theology and pastoral practice should respond to the situations described by Plato (among many others) from the point of view of Catholic teaching. This is an immense task, in the accomplishment of which a theology and pastoral practice deeply influenced by historicism is of little help. A historicist theology, which seems to be the prevailing type of moral theology taught in the United States, is at least partly responsible for the inappropriate silence and unwitting errors of pastors on moral matters.

DR. JOHN M. HAAS

THE SACRAL CHARACTER OF THE PRIEST AS THE FOUNDATION FOR HIS MORAL LIFE AND TEACHING

Holier than thou! —it is an attitude of which no Christian— and certainly no priest—would ever want to be accused. *Holier than thou!* —the expression bespeaks a self-righteousness, a smug haughtiness, entirely incompatible with Christian humility. Jesus reserved his sharpest rebukes not just for those who gave the appearance of rectitude, but also for those who were most careful in their observance of the Law and yet displayed self-satisfaction with their observance. Indeed, our Lord himself was criticized by the religious zealots for healing on the Sabbath. But, as Walter Grundmann points out, Jesus repudiates such apparent piety for it "does not in fact serve God, since it shows contempt for a human being".[1] *Holier than thou!* —a rebuke that ought to make any Christian recoil.

And yet, from another perspective, there is a certain truth to the expression when it is applied to the Catholic priest. He is, quite objectively, holier than a lay Christian. Nevertheless, to avoid justifiable indignation, we must make an immediate clarification as to what is meant when we say that the priest is holier than another Christian.

Inaugral lecture of the John Cardinal Krol Chair in Moral Theology.
[1] Walter Grundmann, *Das Evangelium nach Markus* (Berlin: Evangelische Verlagsanstalt, 1968), 73.

THE CONCEPT OF HOLINESS

The problem naturally arises because of the moral connotations attached to the term *holiness*. If we refer to someone as a holy man or woman, we invariably mean that he or she is a moral person, one for whom we ought to have the highest regard.

But holiness is fundamentally a religious rather than a moral category.[2] Although morality is invariably bound up in our understanding of holiness, it has a certain antecedent sense that seems to have little to do with moral conduct.[3]

Of course holiness properly refers only to God. *Qadosh, Hagios, Sanctus* — the three sacred languages of our religion declare him to be thrice holy. We proclaim the same every single time we plead the eucharistic sacrifice: "Holy, Holy, Holy Lord God of Hosts". He has no equal. He is totally beyond anything we can know or

---

[2] Cf. *agios, Theological Dictionary of the New Testament,* vol. I, ed. Gerhard Kittel (Grand Rapids, Mich.: Wm. B. Eerdmans, 1968); "holiness", *Sacramentum Mundi,* vol. 3, ed. Karl Rahner (New York: Herder and Herder, 1969); "holiness", "holiness (in the Bible)", "holiness, law of", "holiness of God", "holiness of the Church", *The New Catholic Encyclopedia,* vol. VII (New York: McGraw-Hill, 1967); "holy", "consecrate", "sanctify", "saints", "devout", *The New International Dictionary of New Testament Theology,* ed. Colin Brown (Grand Rapids, Mich.: Zondervan, 1967); "heilig", *Theologisches Begriffslexikon zum Neuen Testament,* vol. II (the German original of *The New International Dictionary of New Testament Theology*), ed. Lothar Coenen, Erich Beyreuther and Hans Bietenhard (Wuppertal: Theologischer Verlag Rolf Brockhaus, 1969); "saintete", *Dictionaire de Theologie Catholique,* vol. IV, ed. A. Vacant, E. Mangenot and E. Amann (Paris: Librairie Letouzey et Ane, 1939); "Heiligkeit", *Handbuch Theologischer Grundbegriffe,* vol. I, ed. Heinrich Fries (Munich: Koesel-Verlag, 1962); "Heiligkeit der Kirche", "Heiligkeit (des Menschen)", "Heiligkeit Gottes", *Lexikon für Theologie und Kirche,* vol. V, ed. Josef Hoefer and Karl Rahner (Freiburg: Verlag Herder, 1960).

[3] *Antecedent* is not meant in a temporal sense; instead it has the most basic, fundamental significance of the word *holy.* Rudolf Otto in *The Idea of the Holy* (London: Oxford University Press, 1957) implies that there was a time when an understanding of the holy was devoid of notions of morality and that over time the concept came to be "filled in" with moral content. Otto, however, is not consistent on this point in his own work. Even the most primitive uses of the concept of holiness appear to carry some overtones of morality.

even imagine. His very name is so holy that the pious Jew does not dare even to utter it.[4] In his presence, even the angels cover their faces as they unceasingly sing of his holiness.

We encounter this complete "otherness" of God throughout the Old Testament. It so surpasses any normal human experience that it is baffling, bewildering, stupefying. It is oddly terrifying at the very time that it is enticing. Whatever God in his holiness touches becomes marked out, separated from its surroundings. After the Great Theophany to Moses on its summit, Sinai became the Holy Mountain, so removed from the profane world of creatures that anyone who wandered upon it—man or beast—was also removed from the realm of the profane by being stoned to death.

The priests of the Old Testament handled with great care those things that had been touched with the holiness of God. Meticulous rituals of purification and preparation were observed to spare them the dangerous effects of that holiness. Around the hem of the skirts of the high priest alternated golden bells and blue, purple and scarlet pomegranates so that "its sound shall be heard when he goes into the holy place before the Lord, and when he comes out, lest he die" (Ex 28:35). Fastened to the front of the high priest's turban with blue lace was a shimmering gold plate that bore the words "Holy to the Lord". Such caution was warranted, for, as the author of Hebrews tells us, "it is a fearful thing to fall into the hands of the living God" (Heb 10:31). The Temple itself was fashioned with various courts and chambers leading, as though with ever-increasing sacral

---

[4] When the tetragrammaton was encountered in the Sacred Scriptures, the word *Adonai* was usually substituted for it. In the King James Version, the Revised Standard Version and the New American Bible, whenever the word *LORD* is encountered in all-capital letters, the assumption of the reader may be that the tetragrammaton appears at that point in the Hebrew text. When the Septuagint was read, the word *kyrios* was used in place of the divine name. When *kyrios* was applied in the New Testament to Jesus of Nazareth, a natural association was made with the God of Abraham, Isaac and Jacob for those familiar with the Septuagint. Cf. Reginald H. Fuller, *The Foundations of New Testament Christology* (New York: Charles Scribner's Sons, 1965), 67–72.

intensity, to the Holy of Holies itself, a place of darkness and silence.[5]

The prophets, too, knew of the holiness of God. When Isaiah had his vision in the Temple, he cried out not with joy but with dread: "Woe is me for I am a man of unclean lips!" The all-holy God does not counter this self-assessment of Isaiah; rather, he purifies the prophet by touching a burning coal to his lips (Is 6). In countless other descriptions of encounters with God, holiness refers to that reality of God's "uncreated and totally inaccessible majesty, by force of which everything else stands opposed to him as absolutely unholy".[6] But this holiness is not simply otherness; it is the totality of all conceivable perfections. God's holiness *is* his righteousness, as Isaiah tells us: "The Lord of hosts is exalted in justice and the Holy God shows himself holy in righteousness" (Is 5:16).

HOLINESS APPLIED TO PERSONS

Not only did places and things become holy in a derivative way after God had communicated himself through them; so also did people. On the holy mountain God chose, set apart and made holy an entire people to be a sign of his sovereignty to all the world. They entered into this state through the shedding and sprinkling of sacrificial blood, by which God's covenant with them was ratified and sealed (Ex 20).[7] God had laid claim to them, not because of any moral stature on their part, but because they might serve his purposes: "You shall be to me a kingdom of priests and a holy nation" (Ex 19:6). Their holiness was derived

[5] Yves Congar, *A Gospel Priesthood* (New York: Herder and Herder, 1967), 80–81; David C. Hicks, "Holiness and Its Tokens", *Canadian Journal of Theology* 15 (July–October 1969): 214–26.

[6] Herbert Haag and Paul van Imshoot, *Bibellexikon,* s.v. "heilig", 687. Cf. Manfred Hauke, *Women in the Priesthood?* (San Francisco: Ignatius Press, 1988), 221.

[7] Cf. Congar, *A Gospel Priesthood,* 90.

from God: "You shall be holy; for I the Lord your God am holy" (Lv 19:2).

This holiness was to be manifested in ritual and moral purity. Not only were the sacrifices offered to God by his people to be holy and without blemish, but also the priests who offered them were to be spotless as well—morally, ritually and even physically (Lv 21: 16–24). But the specific cultic, religious significance of holiness cannot be separated from the moral. Even as God on Sinai declared the Israelites to be "a kingdom of priests and a holy nation", he presented to them the Decalogue stating the consequences of and conditions for the new relationship. God's declaration to his chosen recorded in Leviticus—"You shall be holy; for I the Lord your God am holy"—not only makes a statement about God's action on his people, but it also introduces the Holiness Code (Lv 17–26) composed of moral and ritual laws to be observed by God's elect.

But even as the moral significance of holiness reached its apogee in the prophets and the New Testament, the cultic, religious significance was never lost. The one to whom the concept can be most fully applied in all its significations is, of course, Jesus of Nazareth. He is the Holy One of God, *ho hagios tou theou*. He is the perfect one, the New Adam, the new creation, the sacrifice without spot or blemish. As Schnackenburg points out,

> On the basis of Hebrew thought "perfect" (*tamin*) really means "intact", "faultless", "sound" (often used in this sense of the sacrificial animals) and the noun (*tom*) also means "innocence", "purity". The idea is not of perfecting by stages but of the integrity of the whole person who belongs to God.[8]

Jesus therefore is both morally pure, i.e., without sin, and ritually pure in the sense of being the perfect sacrifice offered totally to God. He is the Holy One of God. The New Testament use of *hagios,* "holy", as a designation for Jesus never loses its religious, ritual overtones.

Jesus was consecrated, set apart for the service of God among

[8] Rudolf Schnackenburg, *The Moral Teaching of the New Testament* (New York: The Seabury Press, 1965), 108–9.

our race. As we are told in Hebrews, "Every high priest is taken from among men and made their representative before God, to offer gifts and sacrifices for sins" (Heb 5:1). Yet in Christ we find that an incredible dynamic has taken place; indeed, it would be inconceivable were it not for revelation. By virtue of the hypostatic union, the High Priest Jesus Christ is not simply consecrated and set apart from the profane; he enters into it in its most profound depths. He is not simply Priest; he is the Victim. He is not only the all-holy God; he is completely one with the sinners for whom the sacrifice is offered. In him who is perfectly God and man, the world in its profaneness is sacralized. The One taken from among men is now most intimately with them for he has pitched his tent among them (Jn 1:14). He is *from* God—indeed, he *is* God—but for no other reason than to be *for* us. This High Priest has no other reason for being other than to effect finally, definitively, once and for all, the reconciliation of our fallen race with its creator through the perfect offering of himself on the altar of the Cross.

Every breath he took, every teaching issuing from his mouth, every healing emanating from his touch, every utterance of forgiveness, every slander endured was a manifestation of his priestly mission. The altar of the Cross was the epitome, the apogee, the consummation of his entire priestly life. The all-holy One who dwells in unapproachable light, the Wholly Other upon whom no one can look and live, finally shows himself in his plenitude, dead upon a cross in the place of execution outside the walls of Jerusalem. As the theologian Joseph Ratzinger points out, "to him who renounced all earthly power ..., to him who laid aside the sword and instead of sending others to their death, as earthly kings do, himself went to his death for others, to him who saw the meaning of human existence not in power and self-assertion but in existing utterly for others—who indeed was, as the cross shows, existence for others—to him and to him alone God has said, 'You are my son, today I have begotten you' ".[9]

[9] Joseph Ratzinger, *Introduction to Christianity* (San Francisco: Ignatius Press, 1990), 162–63.

Here we see how misled are those moralizers of the Enlightenment who prefer to point to the teachings of Jesus rather than to Jesus. This is a particular problem in a society as pluralistic as our own, where we seek some common ground in morality for our life together. We see the problem embedded in our national tradition in a Thomas Jefferson editing his own version of the New Testament by eliminating the miraculous acts of Jesus and preserving only his ethical teachings. But the teachings of Jesus cannot be separated from his saving act on Calvary. His entire life, death and Resurrection was his teaching. He left us not merely a code of conduct, not even merely an example of supreme love and sacrifice; he left us a new people born of the blood and water that flowed from his wounded side. He created us "a chosen race, a royal priesthood, a holy nation, a people of his own" (1 P 2:9a).[10] Why? "[So] that [we] may announce the praises of him who called [us] out of darkness into his wonderful light" (1 P 2:9b).

THE CHURCH AS HOLY

There is a sense in which the elect (*eklektoi tou theou*), the Church (*ekklesia*), can be called "holier than thou". As should be abundantly clear by now, this must be in a religious, not a moral, sense. In fact, this is precisely what the elect are as the new "holy nation". They are now the "holy ones" because they have been united with the Holy One of God through baptism. Saint Paul addresses the recipients of his letters as "the saints", "the holy ones" (*hoi hagioi*), but upon reading the epistles it becomes immediately and abundantly clear that he is not praising their high moral qualities. In fact, he chastises them for their rancor and divisiveness and sexual abuses. Yet despite these imperfections,

---

[10] Regarding "a chosen race", cf. Is 43:20–21; "a royal priesthood", cf. Ex 19:6; "a holy nation", cf. Ex 19:6.

they are still the holy ones, the elect of God; and it is this very fact that Saint Paul seizes upon to call them to a life of exemplary—indeed, supernatural—virtue. By virtue of what they are, holy, he calls them to lead holy lives: "I . . . urge you to live in a manner worthy of the call you have received" (Ep 4:1). The call the Christian has received is to be one with Christ, to whom he is joined in baptism. To defile oneself is to defile the Holy One of God with whom the Christian has become one: "Do you not know that your bodies are members of Christ? Shall I then take Christ's members and make them the members of a prostitute? Of course not!" (1 Co 6:15).

There is a dynamic to the Christian life in which the Christian is acted upon, made holy, and in which he acts, sanctifying himself in accord with his status. The same person can be both *holy* (*hagios*) and *righteous* (*dikaios*), but the one term refers to the status given him by God and the other to his own actions. As Gerhard Kittel points out,

> whether under Hellenistic influence or not, the reference of holiness is always to the static morality of innocence rather than to ethical action. But this static morality is closely linked with cultic qualification. For this reason we should never translate *hagiōtes* or *hagios* as morality or moral, since this is to lose the element of the *religiosum*.[11]

The passive nature of holiness and the active nature of righteousness is strikingly captured in the voices of the verb in a passage from the Apocalypse: "Let . . . the righteous still *do* right, and the holy still *be* holy" (Rv 22:11).[12] There is a passivity to the category of holiness that can be seen in the use of such terms as *election* and in such passages as "It was not you who chose me, it was I who chose you" (Jn 15:16). It was in such terms that Hans Urs von Balthasar spoke of his own calling:

---

[11] Gerhard Kittel, ed., *Theological Dictionary of the New Testament,* vol. I (Grand Rapids, Mich.: Wm. B. Eerdmans, 1968), 109.

[12] *Ho dikaios dikaiosunēn poiēsatō eti* (active) *kai ho hagios hagiasthētō eti* (passive).

Even now, thirty years later, I could still go to that remote path in the Black Forest, not far from Basel, and find again the tree beneath which I was struck as by lightning. . . . And yet it was neither theology nor the priesthood which then came into my mind in a flash. It was simply this: you have nothing to choose, you have been called. You will not serve, you will be taken into service.[13]

Religious persons will speak of having been seized or chosen or set apart by the holy God. Morality, on the other hand, requires activity, the self-initiated performance of good deeds. Yet the two are inseparable despite an antecedent quality to election. Thus, the verse "It was not you who chose me, it was I who chose you" concludes with "to go forth and bear fruit".

Despite the supernatural character of the reality under discussion, it conforms with the commonsensical idea contained in the scholastic axiom *agere sequitur esse*. Act follows upon being; a thing acts in accord with its nature. Those who have received the gift of faith and have been endowed with the indelible character of baptism are no longer simply worldly and carnal. They are called apart, consecrated, set aside to redeem that world within which they continue to live. Yet their nature is not destroyed. They have not become angels; they are still men and women. But they are now empowered to do what would have been entirely impossible for them before their election. Their nature has been altered, modified; and they are now to live the life of Jesus Christ himself as his Body in the world. As Saint Paul urged the Roman Christians to live in accord with what they were, he urged them to offer themselves as a living sacrifice, holy and pleasing to God (Rm 12:1).

---

[13] Peter Henrici, "Hans Urs von Balthasar: A Sketch of His Life", *Communio* (Fall 1989), 311.

THE PRIEST AS THE HOLY MAN

All that has preceded does not simply constitute preliminary reflections on the sacral character of the priest as the foundation for his moral life and teaching. Rather, it is integral to the consideration at hand. The idea of the sacred, consecrated person is not alien to the Christian dispensation; it is essential to it. Furthermore, the notion of sacrality extends beyond and indeed even predates the Church. No one should therefore be startled to read in the "Dogmatic Constitution on the Church" from the Second Vatican Council that the common priesthood of all the faithful and the ordained, hierarchical priesthood differ not only in degree, but also in essence (*essentia et non gradu tantum*).[14]

Among the holy people of God, consecrated and conformed to the likeness of Christ, are others who have undergone another consecration, resulting in another, objectively more profound conformity to Christ himself. These are men who, through absolutely no merit of their own, have been chosen and set apart for the service of God. In relation to the laity they have become "holier than thou". Clearly this is not meant in a subjective, moral sense. We know all too painfully, and none more painfully than the man who is a priest, that they are not by any means necessarily "more moral than thou". But they have been set apart, consecrated, ordained, for the service of God and their fellow Christians. To effect what they have been called to do, they have been specially empowered by God. As the Council tells us, "The ministerial priest, by the sacred power (*potestas sacra*) that he has, forms and rules the priestly people; in the person of Christ he effects the eucharistic sacrifice and offers it to God in the name of all the people."[15]

The testimony of Scripture, Tradition and the Church's most recent ecumenical council is quite clear in pointing to a setting

---

[14] *Lumen Gentium,* no. 10.
[15] Ibid.

apart and consecrating of sacred ministers so that their very nature
is modified. Paul describes himself as "a slave of Jesus Christ, called
to be an apostle and set apart" (Rm 1:1). *"Sacerdotes consecrantur"*,
"priests are consecrated", Saint Thomas tells us in the *Summa
Theologica*.[16] And the Council tells us quite unequivocally, *"Presbyteri
consecrantur ut veri sacerdotes Novi Testamenti"*, "Presbyters are consecrated as true priests of the New Testament."[17] Here we find
a link not only with Christ, but even with the Old Testament
sacrifices that prefigured his. Saint Jerome wrote to Evangelus,
"What Aaron and his sons were in the Temple, that are the bishops
and priests of the Church."[18]

Of course what the priest of the New Dispensation performs
far exceeds that of the Old. He pleads before the Father the perfect
sacrifice of Christ himself and brings the benefits of that sacrifice
to the people of God. The priest stands in their midst *in persona
Christi,* acting in the very person of Christ. Because such power
far exceeds man's natural endowments, he must be empowered
from on high, which is what occurred when the apostles were
consecrated and told to offer the Eucharist until our Lord's coming again. This consecration given the priest in ordination is as
permanent as is our baptismal consecration and goes by the technical term *indelible character.*

As the theological virtues of faith, hope and love empower us
to perform supernatural actions of which we would be incapable
without those free gifts from God, so the grace of ordination
enables the priest to perform actions of which a mere man, even a
baptized man, would be incapable. Through that gift he can
transform bread and wine into the food of immortality and forgive the sins of the repentant. As Saint Thomas tells us, "The
works of God are perfect; and consequently whoever receives
power from above receives also those things that render him

---

[16] ST III, 67, 2.

[17] LG, no. 28. Similar statements can be found in *Presbyterorum Ordinis,* nos. 5
and 12.

[18] St. Jerome, Ep. 146 to Evangelus.

competent to exercise that power."[19] The grace of orders confers, Saint Thomas tells us elsewhere, a *virtus instrumentalis,* an instrumental power, not a personal one, which enables the priest to serve the higher purposes to which he has been called.[20] This is the very power of which Paul speaks in his exhortation to his spiritual son, Timothy, "I remind you to stir into flame the gift of God that you have through the imposition of my hands" (1 Tm 1:6).

This *character indelibilis* and the efficacious power of the sacraments *ex opere operato* are neither mark of privilege nor magic, but incomparably precious gifts to the faithful so that they might be assured of the grace of God despite the unworthiness or inattentiveness of the sacred minister. As Josef Pieper points out in an essay titled "What Is a Priest?" the consecrated state is

> an actual, objective attribute which, although it obligates its possessor to live a life worthy of a "servant of the sacred", nevertheless remains in force quite independently of his personal "worthiness". By the same token, the respect which the faithful owe to an "ordained" ("consecrated") priest is not owed to him personally, because of his irreproachable moral conduct or his intellectual and spiritual endowments, but rather to the attribute he receives in the *consecratio.*[21]

By virtue of God's grace and the indelible character the priest now acts, as Saint Paul puts it, *in persona Christi* (2 Co 2:10). Christ's life and ministry are now his life and ministry. As he surrenders his life to Christ's the Lord's promise is fulfilled in him: "[I]t will not be you who speak but the Spirit of your Father speaking through you" (Mt 10:20). The priest does not stand between God and man, but rather mediates Christ immediately to the faithful. The sacramental powers that he has are

---

[19] ST Suppl., 35, 1.

[20] ST III, 65, 5 ad 1. Cf. also *Summa Contra Gentiles,* iv, cap. 74.

[21] Josef Pieper, *Problems of Modern Faith* (Chicago: Franciscan Herald Press, 1985), 68.

Christ's, not his. That is why Saint Thomas refers to them as instrumental rather than personal powers. When the priest administers the sacraments, Christ works in and through him. As the Council pointed out in the "Constitution on the Sacred Liturgy", Christ himself "is present at the sacrifice of the mass ... in the person of the priest".[22] The priest is priest not for himself but for the faithful and, as such, reveals the sublime, self-donating nature of the Trinity itself. As our Holy Father has said, "The priesthood is not ours to do with as we please. . . . Ours is to be true to the one who has called us. The priesthood is a gift to us. But in us and through us the priesthood is a gift to the Church".[23]

SACRAL CHARACTER AS FOUNDATION FOR THE PRIEST'S MORAL LIFE

The holiness of priesthood is a gratuitous gift from God, undeserved and truly incomparable. It has the passive quality of being something granted by God to a man despite his unworthiness. Yet the man is indeed transformed. He receives an indelible character and the grace to live the life that has been granted to him. The priest is patterned after, configured to (*configuratur*) Christ as priest.[24] It is no longer he who lives, but Christ who lives in him.

The priest, then, is to become fully that which he is. He must be subject to the principle of *agere sequitur esse*. The active element of righteousness must become realized as he cooperates with God's grace in living out that which he has become. As we all know, this is manifested publicly and ritually in the holy Mass, to

---

[22] *Sacrosanctum Concilium,* no. 7.

[23] John Paul II, "Address to the Scottish Priests and Men and Women Religious in Edinburgh's Catholic Cathedral" (May 13, 1982). *Origins,* vol. 12, no. 4 (June 10, 1982).

[24] *Presbyterorum Ordinis,* no. 12.

which sacrament the priest is preeminently ordered.[25] Only the priest can assume this role in the Christian community by virtue of God's grace and power.[26] As the Holy Father has pointed out, "the celebrant, by reason of this special sacrament, identifies himself with the eternal high priest, who is both author and principal agent of his own sacrifice in which truly no one can take his place."[27] But the sacrifice of Christ was the total surrender of his life to the Father in the Spirit for his friends as well as the total surrender of his life to his friends for his Father's sake. This is the holiness that comes to mark the life of the priest. The Council tells us that the source of all pastoral charity is the eucharistic sacrifice, for here the priest is most sublimely configured to his Lord. In the words of the Council, "This sacrifice is . . . the center and root of the whole life of the priest, so that the priestly soul strives to make his own what is enacted on the altar of sacrifice".[28]

Through his ordination the priest has entered more fully into the paschal mystery. As Jesus was entirely from God and entirely for us, so the priest is entirely from Christ and entirely for us. He is consumed in his surrender to God and to us faithful. His entire life is an oblation. As with Christ, one cannot separate his person and his work. That which the priest has become defines not only his personhood, but also his activity. By way of analogy, when a man marries he becomes a spouse, irrevocably and forever. Likewise, when a man is consecrated he becomes a priest, irrevocably and forever. A man may walk away from his wife, but he will never cease being her spouse. A man may walk away from the clerical state, but he will never cease being a priest. As the married man witnesses to the world and indeed lives the absolutely indissoluble bond of love that unites Christ to his Church, so the consecrated man witnesses Christ's sacrificial love to the world in the most

[25] Ibid., no. 2.

[26] "The Minister of the Eucharist" (August 6, 1983). *Origins*, vol. 13, no. 14 (September 15, 1983).

[27] John Paul II, "Dominicae Cenae", 8:AAS 72 (1980) 128–29.

[28] *Presbyterorum Ordinis*, no. 14.

intimate way conceivable, by a very transformation of his being. God help any man who would disfigure the face of Christ before the world by betraying his own being, as Christian spouse or as priest.

The priest is configured to Christ and filled with his grace to overflowing. It makes of him more than he could ever hope to be in his natural condition. He has, after all, given himself away entirely. He has given up family, home, possessions, worldly power, not out of denial but out of superabundance. There is no room for such things! In this he imitates Christ. As Josef Ratzinger puts it in another context, "[E]xcess is . . . the real foundation and form of the history of salvation, which in the last analysis is nothing other than the truly breathtaking fact that God, in an incredible outpouring of himself, expends not only a universe but his own self in order to lead man, a speck of dust, to salvation. So excess or superfluity . . . is the real definition or mark of the history of salvation."[29]

The priest's life is one of excess, of generosity. It is generosity, not stinginess, that is the cause of celibacy. We can again see an analogy in marriage. It is not that a married man gives up other women; rather, it is that his whole being is so filled with his beloved that there is no room for other women. It is not that a priest has given up a wife and family; rather, it is that his whole being is so filled with, so configured to Christ that there is no room for anything else. And in surrendering himself to Christ he finds that he, as his Lord, has surrendered himself to everyone he encounters.

The priesthood should consume a priest so that his entire life is an oblation in service to others as was the life of his Lord. He must give everything for it. In Germany, I am told, there stands a most peculiar piano. It is much lower than the conventional piano and has teeth marks deeply set in the woodframe beneath the keys. Beethoven had commissioned the piano to be built for him. This musical genius had given his whole life over to his art. Yet by the

---

[29] Ratzinger, *Introduction to Christianity*, 197.

cruelest of fates this man was losing his hearing and faced the risk of losing touch with the passion of his life, his music. So Beethoven had the piano built so that he could sit on the floor to play. And as he played, he would sink his teeth into the wood, desperately trying to remain in touch with the world of sound that had been his whole life. Here, perhaps, is a simile for the priest whose passion for living the priesthood of Christ should be no less. Just like the Eucharistic Sacrifice, his life ought to be offered in its totality *per Christum et in Christo*, through Christ and in Christ.

Saint Irenaeus wrote of this total giving of self, which is the hallmark of the New Dispensation that he compared with the Old:

> The rite of sacrificial offerings has not been rejected. There were sacrificial offerings then and there are today. There were sacrifices among the [Jewish] people, there are sacrifices in the Church. . . . They consecrated only the tenth of their possessions, but we . . . set apart for the Lord's use all that is ours . . . like that poor widow, the Church, who offered up all her life into the treasury of God.[30]

The priesthood of Christ is a life of total sacrificial service.

A final word on the sacral character of the priest as the foundation for his moral teaching through the witness of his life. One often hears objections today to the fact that the world in general and the faithful in particular expect a higher degree of morality from the priest than they do from others and that this puts unjustifiable pressures and demands on the priest. After all, we are told, he is a man like any other, suffering from all the same weaknesses and temptations as any other man suffers. All this is true, of course. And all are called to the same degree of personal sanctity, priests and laity alike. But it is also true that those who have assumed a public ministry, which is what the priesthood is, those who have been publicly and sacramentally configured to the

---

[30] Irenaeus, *Adv. Haer.*, IV.

priestly life of Christ, are expected to manifest that life in a publicly more intense way.

The laity are those Christians hidden in the world transforming it from within. The priests are those who conspicuously manifest Christ in our midst. This is one reason that, in imitation of Christ, priests do not marry, they do not have families, they do not have a home, they do not do their own will but rather that of the One who sends them to one assignment after another. They wear some external mark of who they are so that they are recognized by friend and foe alike, by benefactor and suppliant alike, as priests of God. This is one of the prices that they pay for making of their lives an oblation offered up for the salvation of the world. Thus, when they fail the sacred trust, when they betray their sacral character as a total offering to God, the price exacted is often excruciating, not only for the priest but for the faithful as well.

Just as the failings of a priest can weaken the entire Body of Christ, so too can his virtue strengthen it. But it is important to understand how the grace of God works so that no priest is ever lulled into a false sense of security by thinking that the sacrament of orders confers in some magical way a greater ability to lead the moral life. The only way in which one can become moral is by doing the good that one ought to do and by avoiding moral evil. Nothing else works. One may consume all the communions one can. One may celebrate Mass every day of his priestly life. But unless the priest chooses and does that which is moral, he will not become virtuous. The sacrament of orders empowers a priest to be and to do that which he would be incapable of in his natural state—that is, to act sacramentally *in persona Christi,* to effect God's saving action in the world. With the sacrament of orders God will also provide the graces necessary for the priest to live in conformity with his nature. But the priest must cooperate with the graces given. The only way he can become moral is by acting morally.

If on the natural plane one is given over to acts of unchastity, for example, an infusion of supernatural grace will not make it any easier to act chastely. Grace makes it possible to perform supernatural acts, and it increases our love for God so that we will more readily do whatever is necessary to please him, but it does not make it easier to perform morally righteous acts if one is habituated to vice.[31] Acts of chastity will not become easier except through repetition. The natural moral virtues must be built up in the priest by the performance, with God's help, of virtuous acts. That is why it is so critically important that the priest heed the exhortation of Saint Paul: "Finally, brothers, whatever is true, whatever is honorable, whatever is just, whatever is pure, whatever is lovely, whatever is gracious, if there is any excellence and if there is anything worthy of praise, think about these things. Keep on doing what you have learned and received and heard and seen in me" (Ph 4:8).

Yet despite the call to sanctity, despite his sacral character, the priest *will* fall. There is but one perfect man, and that is Jesus Christ. "All have sinned and fallen short of the glory of God" (Rm 3:23). "If we say, 'We are without sin', we deceive ourselves, and the truth is not in us" (1 Jn 1:8). Scripture is filled with ample examples of those who have been called by God and who have fallen. The human frailty of priests should surprise no one: of such is the kingdom of heaven; it is for such that Christ came. As Henri de Lubac points out in *The Splendor of the Church,* the Church is holy, not because it is composed of flawless people, but because the Lord bestows holiness on her as an entirely unmerited gift.[32] Indeed, in his weakness the priest finds added strength in the ministry he offers God's people. What is often seen as scandal — that is, the sinfulness of the Church and her ministers — can be a source of comfort. "I must admit", writes Cardinal Ratzinger, "that to me this unholy holiness of the Church has in itself something infinitely comforting about it. Would one not be bound to despair in face of a holiness that was spotless and

---

[31] Cf. E. Towers, "Sanctifying Grace", in *The Teaching of the Catholic Church,* ed. George D. Smith (New York: Macmillan, 1960), 572–75. Cf. also T. E. Flynn, "The Supernatural Virtues", ibid., 629–30.

[32] Henri de Lubac, *The Splendor of the Church* (San Francisco: Ignatius Press, 1986), esp. chapter III, 85–125.

could only operate on us by judging us and consuming us by fire?"[33]

The sacrament of confession is for the priest as well as the laity. There, on his knees as penitent, the priest enacts his ministry and realizes it as surely and in as sacrificial a manner as it is when he stands at the altar of God. The late Spanish priest José Maria Escriva, in the briefest of reflections, integrated the penitential, sacrificial, sacramental and eucharistic elements that comprise the life of the priest in this context: "In the Sacrament of Penance it is Jesus who forgives us. Christ's merits are applied to us there. It is for love of us that he is on the Cross with his arms stretched out, stitched to the wood more by the Love he has for us than by the nails."[34] The priest, like any other Christian, stands in need of Christ's forgiveness and should avail himself of the sacramental, reconciling ministry of his fellow priests on a regular and quite frequent basis. He, above all men, must be sober and vigilant, for the devil, as a roaring lion, finds few prey so tantalizing as a priest of God (1 P 5:8).

THE SACRAL CHARACTER AS FOUNDATION FOR MORAL TEACHING

As has been noted, the person of the priest is not to be separated from his work as teacher and preacher. The preeminent way in which the priest teaches, of course, is through the example of his life. But the priest also has the charge to teach in a more formal way as well.

It must be remembered that what the priest teaches is not his own. He only hands on that which he has received. In fact, the priest is obliged by virtue of the nature of his vocation to teach Jesus Christ and him crucified. The whole of faith, the delibera-

---

[33] Ratzinger, *Introduction to Christianity*, 265.
[34] José Maria Escriva, *The Forge* (New York: Scepter, 1988), 87.

tions of the councils, the sacred science of the doctors of the Church, the magisterial pronouncements throughout the ages — all center on one historical person, Jesus of Nazareth, to whose likeness the priest is conformed. If he is to *live* Jesus Christ, how could he do anything other than to *teach* Jesus Christ, and specifically as Jesus Christ is known and understood by his own Body, the Catholic Church, filled with his Spirit leading her into all truth?

The teaching office, as well as the sacramental office, serves no purpose other than to build up the Body of Christ in its service to God and the world. The priest is the servant of the Word of God, which he is to proclaim with fidelity to those who have been entrusted with its true interpretation.[35] "The task of priests", said the Council, "is not to teach their own wisdom but God's Word."[36] This task is no less his as priest than is the offering of the eucharistic sacrifice. Both are inseparably linked. Origen wrote of the joining of the two:

> You know, you who are accustomed to assist at the divine mysteries, with what religious care, when you receive the Lord's body, you watch to see that not the smallest particle may fall. . . . You would feel guilty, and rightly so, if that were to happen by your neglect. Then, . . . how should it be a less grave fault to neglect the word of God than to neglect his body?[37]

At this point note must be taken of a particular crisis within the priesthood today in the area of teaching, and that is the unfounded timidity of many priests to teach the hard doctrines of Christ, whom they represent. It is certainly out of a sense of compassion that many draw back from a clear articulation of some of the more severe demands of the Gospel. But it is a misbegotten compassion, for it ultimately does service neither to the people of God nor to the world at large. As Paul VI said, and John Paul II

---

[35] DV, no. 10. Cf. also Pius XII, *Humani Generis* (August 12, 1950).
[36] *Presbyterorum Ordinis,* no. 4.
[37] Origen, *In Exod.,* hom. 13.3.

has reiterated, "To diminish in no way the saving teaching of Christ constitutes an eminent form of charity for souls."[38]

Divorce and remarriage is no option for Christians. Marriage is no option for an ordained priest. Contraception is objectively and intrinsically immoral, and abortion is so vile and contemptuous of human goods that it ought not even to be mentioned among us, much less contemplated and carried out. Homosexual acts are disordered, an offense against God and a disservice to oneself. Has the teaching on these evils become equivocal in recent years because priests are afraid of hurting people's feelings? Or do they fear for themselves the displeasure and perhaps rejection that such teaching might engender? Or do they no longer believe that God has spoken to us clearly through the Scriptures and the Church's Magisterium? Whatever its source, such a course would bode ill for their priesthood and for the people priests have been called to serve.

Saint Thomas tells us in the *Summa Contra Gentiles* that God is offended by us only when we act against our own good. The Church warns us against any of the acts just mentioned because each is contrary to our own good. They all constitute a disordered choice for a supposed good in such a way that we close ourselves off to the potentials for self-realization and happiness that are truly meant to be ours. Through bad choices we constitute ourselves as bad people, which means unhappy people, miserable people, alienated, isolated, yes, damned people. Our Lord wept over Jerusalem: "If you only knew what makes for peace" (Lk 19:42). But of course we now do know. It is a life in conformity with the mind of Christ as shown to us by his Catholic Church. Only this can bring true peace.

Here we can see, too, that the task of the priest is not just to serve the household of faith, building up the Body of Christ; it is also to be at the service of society by working for its conversion through his moral teaching and guidance.

The task today is monumental and fraught with danger. The

---

[38] Paul VI, *Humanae Vitae*, no. 29. John Paul II, *Familiaris Consortio*, no. 33.

spiritual, moral and cultural crises facing the formerly Christian societies of the West weigh heavily upon our current pope. But the crises of our day are fundamentally crises of saints, i.e., those called to be holy. The moral disorder results from a spiritual disorder, and both play on one another, as Saint Paul tells us in the first chapter of Romans.

The forging of a new Christian society is going to be no easy task. It will require sacrifice, social opprobrium, perhaps even martyrdom in some fashion or another. But then, it is just of such stuff that the priesthood of Jesus Christ consists. For the task to be accomplished the priest must live his priesthood to the utmost, withholding nothing. A new culture cannot be forged without the greatest effort, as Virgil remarks in the famous line *"Tantae molis erat Romanam condere gentem"* — "Such a toil it was to found the Roman people!" Much more will this observation apply to the priest of Jesus Christ as he labors with the entire mystical Body to bring forth a new Christian civilization as we enter the third millenium of the New Dispensation.

But the priest can do this only by being what he is — a priest — unequivocally, unashamedly, with total dedication. The priest, as a sacral person, stands in sharp contrast to the accepted and often morally numbing conventions of the society in which he finds himself. His very manner of life shocks and confounds those around him. Nonbelievers — and, indeed, many believers — find it simply incredible that he forever renounces his right to marry and establish a family. Even more incredible in contemporary American society, he has given up any use of his sexual faculties. He does not accumulate wealth. He does not seek political power. Even his clothing is odd, peculiar, out of the ordinary. He is a man who lives at the margins and in the interstices of conventional life. Strangely enough, despite his oddity, or perhaps because of it, even social anthropologists recognize the socially integrating function of such sacral, "liminal", one might almost say "numinous", individuals.[39]

[39] Cf. Victor W. Turner, *The Ritual Process* (Chicago: Aldine, 1969).

The priest constitutes an intensification of the sacred within the Christian body as the Body of Christ brings the sacred into the profane for its sanctification. Pius XII describes this dynamic in his encyclical *Mediator Dei:*

> In the same way, actually, that Baptism is the distinctive mark of all Christians, and serves to differentiate them from those who have not been cleansed in this purifying stream and consequently are not members of Christ, the Sacrament of Holy Orders sets the priest apart from the rest of the faithful who have not received this consecration.[40]

In his sacrality that is in no way separate from his humanity the priest points to the holiness of God, who is the source of all morality. By so doing he forever calls the world to acknowledge, whether they are of the Christian faith or not, that there is an objective moral order and that there one day will be a judgment for our chosen actions.

There are those today who would eliminate distinctions between the sacred and the profane. Sanctuaries are to be replaced with eucharistic assembly halls. Priests offering sacrifice are to be replaced with functionaries, presidents, enablers. All of life is to be holy. All people are equally holy. No day is more sacred than another. Yet without ferial days there are no holy days. Without ordinary time there is not the extraordinary time of Christmas or Easter. Without fasts there are no feasts. Rather than all becoming holy through such attempts at eliminating the distinction between the sacred and the profane, all become desacralized in a pervasive, deadening secularism. Declaring no person, place or thing to be in any way distinct from another in terms of its relationship to God results in no thing and no place and no one being sacred. Even innocent human life, which until recently continued to be imbued with a sacredness that left it inviolable, is no longer sacred in our secularized society.

The sacral character of priests reminds us all of the Source of

---

[40] Pius XII, *Mediator Dei,* no. 43, November 20, 1947 (Boston: St. Paul Editions, nod.) 21–22.

our life. Such a presence and such a power are absolutely essential to the task of transforming the world. Strangely, even the profane, secular world cannot come properly into its own without the sacred. Without the holy, the profane, secular world degenerates into profanity and secularism. Without the supernatural, the natural degenerates into the unnatural. It is a dynamic built into the very order of things that is absolutely unavoidable. It is unnatural for man to be immoral, for him not to seek his own good. But that is exactly what happens when he loses sight of the sacred. Without the supernatural, the human person degenerates into the unnaturalness of immorality. Man cannot even be natural without God.

So the priest, by being intensely and clearly a priest, will help the layman and laywoman in their baptismal consecration be even more perfectly lay, which is their vocation. As the sacred is more clearly sacred, the secular will be more clearly and properly itself. The secular has its own appropriate sphere in which the laity carry out their affairs without ecclesiastical interference because it is their task to seek their own personal sanctity as laity, not clerics. The profane is, after all, not a realm devoid of God. All is God's. There is no place where one might escape him. The profane is not evil and destitute of God but rather, as the word indicates, that area before the temple, *pro fanum,* where the common affairs of daily life are carried out. So with a clear demarcation from the temple, the profane is able to be more fully that which it ought to be in its own right, providing the context for the moral life of the ordinary Christian with a priestly soul who thereby transforms the world from within.

The Blessed Virgin Mary, though numbered among the laity, can nonetheless provide the model for the moral life of the priest. This is because the priest's life is based on the paschal mystery of Jesus Christ, i.e., on our Lord's entire life of sacrificial service, which is imprinted on the priest in his sacral character. No one has patterned the paschal mystery more perfectly than our Blessed Mother herself, who totally joined her life to that of her Son in his sacrifice. She did this from the first moment she declared, "Be it done unto me according to your word." Her sacrifice unfolded throughout her life with his own sacrifice. It can be seen when she presented her Son in the Temple. The true offering she made on that occasion was not the two young turtledoves but her acceptance of the sufferings that would accompany her Son's ministry as foretold by Simeon. The Jesuit Jean Galot describes its significance beautifully: "We have here a first offering of the sacrifice that redeems, a mother's sacrifice which precedes and already implies Jesus' own priestly offering of himself still to come. This consecration transcends ritual formalism; it bespeaks a personal commitment."[41] This consecration was a surrender to a life of sacrificial service in imitation of her Divine Son. As Saint Augustine said, "Because there is a sacrifice, there is a priesthood."[42]

[41] Jean Galot, *Theology of the Priesthood* (San Francisco: Ignatius Press, 1985), 39.
[42] *Confessions* X, 43, 69.

HOMILY AT ST. CHARLES BORROMEO SEMINARY

for the Third Sunday of the Year, January 21, 1990

The reading from the first letter of Saint Paul to the Corinthians that we have just heard has a startling pertinence for us. It is true that Paul speaks to the community of Corinth from a time long past and that he admonishes it in conscience concerning all those things found there in opposition to true Christian living. Yet we sense right away that these words concern not just the problems of a Christian community from long ago; they meet us here and now, today. When Paul speaks to the Corinthians, he is speaking to us and pointing at the wounds of our lives in the Church today. We are in danger, just like the Corinthians, of tearing apart the Church with partisan conflicts while each of us develops his own ideas about Christianity. Thus it happens that our rights become more important than God's claim upon us, than our being right or just in his sight. Our own ideas obscure the Word of the living God while the Church recedes behind the development of parties that grow out of our own thinking. The similarity between the situation of the Corinthian Church and our own should not be overlooked. But is not Paul's intention simply to describe a situation; he speaks to us in order to rouse our consciences and to direct us once more toward the true integrity and unity of Christian living. And so we have to ask him: What is really wrong with our way of living? What must we do so that we might be not the party of

Paul or Apollos or Cephas or even the party of Christ but rather the Church of Jesus Christ? What is the difference between being a Christian group or party and being his living Church?

Let us try, first of all, to understand what was truly happening in Corinth and what is constantly threatening to occur anew in history because of the very same human perils. The distinction in question could perhaps be formulated in these words: If I stand up for a party, then it becomes my party. The Church of Jesus Christ, however, is never my Church; it is always his Church. The essence of conversion consists in the fact that I no longer seek for myself a party looking after my interests and corresponding to my likes, but that I place myself in his hands and become his, a member of his Body, the Church. Let us try to look at this a little more closely. The Corinthians perceived in Christianity an interesting religious theory that was in keeping with their hopes and expectations. They chose what suited them, and they chose it in a form in accord with their own likes. When one's own desires and wishes are decisive, however, divisions will have already set in, for those to be pleased are many and opposed one to the other. From such ideological options a club or a circle of friends or a party may arise, but not a Church that overcomes the differences between people and unites them in the peace of God. Personal preference is the principle upon which a club is formed; however, the principle upon which the Church is based is obedience to the Lord's call, as we see in today's Gospel: "He called them and at once, leaving the boat and their father, they followed Him" (Mt 4:21f.).

And so we have come to the decisive point: Faith is not the choice of whatever program appeals to me; nor is it the joining of some fraternal club where I feel I am understood. Faith means conversion that transforms me and my preferences or at least allows my desires and wishes to become secondary. Faith reaches down to a much greater depth than a decision binding me to some party. Its power to transform goes so far that Scripture calls it a new birth (cf. 1 P 1:3, 23). Here we come to an important insight that we will have to consider in greater depth, for this is where the heart of the problems concerning us today in the Church lies hidden. It is difficult for us to conceive of the Church in any way other than the model of a self-governing society that applies the mechanisms of majority and minority in such a fashion as to assume a form agreeable to all its members. It is difficult for us to understand faith in any way other than a decision for something that pleases us and that we might like to promote. In every case, though, it is always ourselves and only ourselves who are the active parties. We make the Church; we try to improve it and to arrange it like a comfortable house. We hope to offer programs and ideals that are acceptable to as many as possible. We simply no longer take it for granted in the modern world that God himself is active, that he is at work. But it is exactly here that we take the plunge with the Corinthians: we substitute the Church with a party and the faith with a party program. The circle of one's private world opens not at all.

Perhaps now we can understand a little better the turning point that faith implies—the about-face, the conversion lying within it: I recognize that God himself speaks and acts, that there is not just what is ours but what is his. But if that is true, if we are not the only ones who can pick and choose and act, if he speaks and acts too, then everything is different. I have to obey; I must follow him even if he leads me where I do not want to go (Jn 21:18). And then it makes sense; indeed, it is necessary to let my own preferences go, to renounce my desires and follow him who alone can show the way to true life, for he himself is the Life (Jn 14:6). This following of him, which is marked by the sign of the Cross, is what Paul ultimately had in mind as an answer to the division of the Corinthians into parties when he stated (10:17): "I give up my own desire and submit myself to Him. It is just in this way, though, that I become free for the truest slavery is that of being imprisoned in the circle of our own desires".

All of this has very serious consequences for the priestly ministry. The priest must be attentive and careful that he is not creating his own church. Paul anxiously examines his conscience as to how people could come to the point of making out of Christ's Church a religious party in his name. He assures himself and the Corinthians that he has done everything to avoid the establishment of bonds that might obscure communion with Christ. One who was converted by Paul does not become an adherent of Paul but of Christ, a member of the one, common Church that is ever the same "whether now Paul or Apollos or Cephas" (1 Co 3:22). Whether this one or that one: "You are Christ's and Christ is God's" (1 Co 3:23).

It is worth the effort to look up the text and to reflect carefully upon all that Paul has written on this point, for here the essence of the priestly ministry is presented with a lucidity that tells us in practical terms and beyond all theorizing what we have to do and what we have to let go:

> What, after all, is Apollos and what is Paul? They are servants who brought the faith to you. . . . I did the planting, Apollos did the watering, but God gave the growth. Neither the planter nor the waterer matters—only God who makes things grow. It is all one who does the planting and who does the watering . . . we are fellow workers with God; you are God's farm, God's building.
>
> (1 Co 3:5-9)

In many Protestant churches of Germany there was and is the custom of announcing the preacher and leader in bulletins for religious services. Behind such names religious parties often conceal themselves: each person may attend the religious service where those of like mind will gather. Unfortunately something similar has begun to occur in Catholic communities too, but this implies that the Church has disappeared behind various parties and that ultimately we are giving attention to human opinions and are no longer listening to the common Word of God, which transcends all of us and whose guarantor is the one Church. Only the unity of the Church's faith and its binding force upon each one assure us that we are not following human opinions and adhering to self-created parties but are uniting ourselves to the Lord in obedience to him. There is great danger today that the Church may disintegrate into religious parties who rally around individual teachers or preachers. Thus it can be said again: I am of Apollos, I am Paul's, I am Peter's; and thus Christ is turned into a party. The standard for priestly ministry is found in self-sacrifice in submission to the word of Jesus: "My teaching is not from Myself" (Jn 7:16). Only if we can say that in all truthfulness are we the "fellow workers with God" who plant and water and thus become sharers in his own work. If men call upon us to witness and pit our Christianity against that of others, this must ever be an occasion for us to examine our consciences. We do not proclaim ourselves but him. This calls for humility on our part, the cross of discipleship. But this is exactly what frees us and renders our service rich and fruitful. For if we proclaim ourselves, we remain shut within our poor and wretched selves and draw others along the same way. If we proclaim him, we become "fellow workers with God" (1 Co 3:9); and what could be more beautiful or liberating than that?

Let us ask the Lord for the grace to recognize anew the joy of this calling. Then will the word of the prophet prove true in our midst, that Word that is ever fulfilled as Christ passes through the nations: "The people who lived in darkness have seen a great light.... People delight in its approach, like those who make merry at harvest time, like those who are joyful when prizes are shared" (Is 9:1–3; cf. Mt 4:15). Amen.

INDEX

ABBREVIATIONS

AAS   *Acta Apostolicae Sedis*

DV   *Dei verbum:* The Dogmatic Constitution on Divine Revelation (1965)

GS   *Gaudium et spes:* The Pastoral Constitution on the Church in the Modern World (1975)

LG   *Lumen gentium:* The Dogmatic Constitution on the Church (1964)

PL   *Patrologia Latina,* ed. J. P. Migne, Paris, 1844–64.

ST   Thomas Aquinas. *Summa Theologica*

ThWNT   *Theologisches Wörterbuch zum Neuen Testament,* ed. G. Kittel. Stuttgart, 1933–